THE DEAF CHILD
IN CARE

PUBLISHED BY

BRITISH AGENCIES FOR

ADOPTION & FOSTERING

11 SOUTHWARK STREET

LONDON SE1 1RQ

© BAAF 1990

ISBN 0 903534 86 X

DESIGNED BY ANDREW HAIG

TYPESET BY ETHNOGRAPHICA LTD

PRINTED AND BOUND IN ENGLAND

The views expressed in this publication are those of the authors and not necessarily those of British Agencies for Adoption & Fostering.

DISCUSSION SERIES: 13

The deaf child in care

◆

*Bridget Warr and
a British Deaf Association
working party*

BRITISH AGENCIES FOR
ADOPTION & FOSTERING

For the late
Claire Brooke-Hughes OBE

Contents

Acknowledgements

This book could not have been written without the co-operation of deaf and hearing foster and adoptive parents, social workers in the deaf and child care fields, schools and units for deaf children, voluntary agencies, local authorities and the wider Deaf Community. We are grateful for the advice, opinions and information they offered so willingly.

Special thanks are due to contributing authors, other than members of the working party, namely Dr Susan Gregory, Senior Lecturer in the Faculty of Social Sciences, Open University, Liz Scott-Gibson, Director of Sign Language Services, The British Deaf Association, and Susanne Turfus, Deputy Director, Yorkshire Residential School for the Deaf.

Finally, our thanks to Joan Turner and Bob Peckford whose particular commitment and effort ensured completion of the work and to the Telethon Trust for funding this publication.

Members of the British Deaf Association working party

Bridget Warr (Chair), Assistant Director, BAAF (to January 1989)

Joan Turner (Secretary to the working party), formerly Senior Social Worker with Deaf People, London Borough of Camden

Bob Peckford, Development Officer, The British Deaf Association (BDA)

Terry Riley, deaf foster parent and BDA Executive Councillor

Rosalind Wyman, adoptive mother and Head, Family Centre, Ealing, National Deaf-Blind and Rubella Association (SENSE)

Jeff Loffill, Social Worker with Deaf People, North Yorkshire Social Services Department

Carlo Laurenzi, Health and Social Services Officer, National Deaf Children's Society (NDCS)

Bess Garnett, foster mother

Mary Jobbins, Social Services Inspector, Department of Health (Observer)

A note on terminology: 'deaf' or 'Deaf'?

To the general reader, the term 'deaf' may seem to mean only the condition of 'not hearing'. However, as we shall see, particularly in Chapters 6 and 7, it is not so simple.

Since the 1960s, studies of indigenous Sign Languages (eg British Sign Language) and their deaf users have led to a greater understanding of this group of deaf people as a linguistic and cultural minority – the Deaf Community.

Padden and Humphries in *Deaf in America: voices from a culture*[1] describe how a convention proposed by James Woodward in 1982[2] uses 'the lowercase *deaf* when referring to the audiological condition of not hearing, and the uppercase *Deaf* when referring to a particular group of deaf people who share a (Sign) Language and a culture. The members of this group have inherited their Sign Language, use it as a primary means of communication among themselves, and hold a set of beliefs about themselves and their connection to the larger society. We distinguish them from, for example, those who find themselves losing their hearing because of illness, trauma or age; although these people share the condition of not hearing, they do not have access to the knowledge, beliefs, and practices that make up the culture of Deaf people.'

Lawson writing in *Perspectives on British Sign Language and Deafness*[3] has described membership of the British Deaf Community in similar terms.

The distinction between Deaf and deaf is not simply a matter of semantics or academic theory; for Deaf people it is central to the question of self-identity and is underlined by the way in which British Sign Language and other Sign Languages distinguish between those who perceive themselves as members of the Deaf Community and those who do not.

However, whilst the distinction is helpful, it is not sufficiently developed to determine clearly the status of some groups. Padden and Humphries raise a question which is particularly relevant to this book: '... consider deaf children from hearing families who encounter Deaf people and their culture outside the family. At what point are they said to have adopted the conventions of the culture and become Deaf?'

There are similar difficulties in applying the distinction in Chapter 5 of this book which reports research studies on deaf children of deaf parents. The criteria for inclusion in these studies was audiological rather than cultural deafness; so although the vast majority of parents discussed would be Deaf, the group inevitably includes a small number who do not perceive themselves as members of the Deaf Community.

For this reason we have chosen in the following chapters to apply the term Deaf (with an uppercase D) *only* where we are clear that the definition quoted above is applicable. The lowercase deaf, therefore, may be used either in a generic sense to include Deaf and deaf; to refer to those deaf people without access to the language and culture of the Deaf Community; or to those whose status in relation to that Community is either unclear or unresolved.

References

1 Padden C and Humphries T *Deaf in America: voices from a culture* Cambridge, Mass: Harvard University Press, 1988.

2 Woodward J *How you gonna get to Heaven if you can't talk to Jesus? – on depathologizing deafness* Maryland, USA: T J Publishers, 1982.

3 Lawson L 'The role of Sign in the Deaf Community' in Woll B, Kyle J and Deuchar M (eds) *Sign Language and Deafness* Croom Helm, 1981.

1 Introduction

The dramatic progress made in the last two decades in the placement of children with special needs in new families has to some extent passed the Deaf Community by. Deaf children in care are less likely than their hearing peers to be in foster or prospective adoptive homes and more likely to be in residential schools.

There are, of course, a number of reasons for this, some understandable (some would even say correct) and others less so. Many of the issues are rooted in the difficulties of communication between hearing and deaf people. Since profound deafness is found only in one in a thousand children, many of the workers in the caring services have little or no direct experience of meeting the needs of a deaf child and are therefore likely to have limited understanding of the implications of deafness.

There is still, sadly, a real risk of the child's deafness becoming a barrier beyond which the social worker is unable to see. The lack of familiarity with the issues and communication problems can render a 'mainstream' child care social worker ill-equipped to make the best plans for a deaf child. There is a national shortage of social workers with deaf people and many of them lack child care expertise. Since 1984 a quarter of all advertised posts for social workers with deaf people have remained unfilled. Of those appointed only two thirds are qualified social workers and only one third are qualified and experienced workers with deaf people.[1]

The problems faced by deaf children are faced also by adult members of the Deaf Community. Traditionally, deaf adults have not readily been considered as potential foster or adoptive parents, and the few who have made (or attempted to make) applications to adopt or foster have typically met with rejection. The number of deaf foster or adoptive parents in Britain is very small, but the reason for this is not lack of parenting skills among the Deaf Community.

Many deaf adults have skills and experience in parenting which would make them highly suitable foster or adoptive parents. In addition they have direct experience of coping with deafness and with the prejudice and ignorance deaf people meet daily. They have communication skills which deaf children need to develop in order to maximise their potential. In short, there are many members of the Deaf Community who would provide excellent care for deaf children, but only a few have been given the opportunity to do so. In the meantime deaf children are waiting for families or are inappropriately placed in residential schools, children's homes or ill-equipped hearing families. Many of the children have more than one disability, and as with other areas of child care, black children are over-represented.

Experience has shown how all children benefit from a secure and loving family. Deaf children and those with multiple disabilities are no exception. It is, therefore, important that more active steps are taken to find new families for the deaf children who need them, and the Deaf Community must be seen as a potential recruiting ground.

More deaf people could also offer other forms of informal help and support to deaf children and be encouraged to make their experience and skills available to support hearing families with a deaf foster or adoptive child.

In 1987 the British Deaf Association (BDA) set up a multi-disciplinary working party to examine the problems of deaf children in care. Among the members of the working party were representatives of the BDA, British Agencies for Adoption and Fostering (BAAF), the National Deaf Children's Society (NDCS), the National Deaf-Blind and Rubella Association (SENSE), adoptive parents, local authority social workers and the Department of Health. The working party consulted with deaf and hearing foster and adoptive parents, deaf young people, social workers in the child care and deaf fields, schools for deaf children, voluntary agencies, medical experts, all local authorities and the wider Deaf Community through group meetings, letters, club meetings and questionnaires. It drew on research in the United Kingdom and USA and on the results of surveys conducted by the NDCS in 1977 and the National Foster Care Association (NFCA) in 1981.

This book is one of the outcomes of that work. It is intended for those in the helping services who wish to provide the best care for deaf children who are temporarily or permanently unable to live with their own families. It explains the definitions of deafness and gives factual information about its causes and about ways of assessing and meeting deaf children's educational and other needs. It also describes the adoption and fostering services and support systems available to deaf children and adults.

We hope that the book will help managers and practitioners in the social services to reach a better understanding of the circumstances surrounding deaf children and adults, black and white, in British society; of the particular benefits which deaf families can bring to adoption and fostering; and of the support systems needed for deaf children and deaf foster and adoptive parents.

A representative of the working party was granted leave to attend a wardship hearing in the high court relating to a three-year-old profoundly deaf child. The case illustrated many of the contentious issues involved in the placement of deaf children in substitute families. A central issue was the question of communication methods and their implications for the child's future care. The judge commented that he had approached the issue of communication methods ' ... with considerable diffidence because I am conscious that, in the course of the hearing, I have had no more than an intelligent introduction to what is a very controversial subject'.

Commenting on a report from an expert witness which indicated that it was unlikely that a girl with this degree of hearing loss could achieve meaningful oral communication, the judge said ' ... on the basis of the statistics that she [the expert witness] has considered and her own personal experience, I think she would possibly agree that the chance that the Ward might be able to communicate orally cannot be excluded wholly, but in terms of making practical decisions, the possibility is so remote that it is necessary to disregard it'.

The judge acknowledged the 'conventional wisdom that the years between three and four are very important years of development and, if a child's communication is restricted during that period and her understanding is restricted because of the means of communication with her, the ultimate result may be greatly to her disadvantage'. He also saw the need for 'a close marriage between the kind of education that the girl will receive at school and the kind of communication she will receive at home'. He gave leave to place the child with long-term foster parents and expressed the hope that the placement would be with the preferred couple – one of two couples available where at least one of the parents was deaf and both were fluent in Sign Language.

It is BAAF's contention that every child has the right to grow up in a family and that a child's needs are best met in such an environment. Deaf children are no different from hearing ones in this respect and we should surely accept no compromise. The communication needs of a deaf child require special attention. Deaf adults or families with other deaf children are often well equipped to help with this.

In view of the number of deaf children who are needing new families and the even fewer number of deaf families currently approved to foster or adopt, it makes sense that a central 'clearing house' should be used in order to maximise each child's chance of a family. BAAF's family placement exchange operates for exactly that purpose and should therefore be consulted by a social worker responsible for the placement of a deaf child or for the recruitment of a deaf family.

Deaf people who identify with the Deaf Community do not seek segregation. They live and work in a hearing world. They have hearing work-mates, friends and neighbours and manage the challenges and difficulties which deafness presents in the daily experience of life in a hearing-oriented environment. However, they also wish to be accepted as Deaf people who value their membership of a Deaf linguistic and cultural minority. That is why they resist pressures to assimilate – they do not want to be viewed as 'slightly deficient examples of hearing people'.

References

1   Smallridge P and Peckford B 'Hearing aides' *Social Services Insight* Vol 2 No 35, 1987.

2 Deaf children in care – the current situation

To gain some insight into the numbers and needs of deaf children in care, their placements and the experience of their carers, the British Deaf Association working party reviewed existing research, undertook two surveys and held a series of consultations.

Surveys by the National Deaf Children's Society (NDCS) in 1977[1] and the National Foster Care Association (NFCA) in 1981 (unpublished)[2] reported the responses of local authorities to questionnaires on different aspects of foster care. Both these surveys and our own questionnaire (1989) to social services departments and voluntary agencies sought details of the numbers of deaf and hearing-impaired children in care. Although comparisons are difficult because of incomplete responses and the lack of definitions of the terms 'deaf' (NDCS) and 'totally deaf' and 'hard of hearing' (NFCA), each survey confirms the relatively small number of children involved.

Informed sources had suggested to the working party that it would find that a high proportion of deaf children in care had additional disabilities and that a significant number were from ethnic minorities. To test these predictions and to find out whether such factors, if present, would influence the availability of substitute family care, we included relevant questions in the questionnaire.

In January 1989 BAAF circulated a questionnaire (see Appendix II) to all 127 social services authorities in Great Britain. Responses were obtained from 69 (54 per cent). Thirty-four local authorities submitted 'nil' returns and 35 recorded having a total of 36 profoundly deaf and 34 partially hearing children in care (Table 1).

Despite the limited response to our questionnaire, Table 2 reinforces the view that a significant proportion (over one third of the total) of deaf and partially hearing children had additional disabilities.

The information available on ethnic background (Table 3) indicated that only ten of the children were black. However, this may be due to the low response rate and/or the lack of returns from areas of the country with larger ethnic minority populations.

Table 1

Deaf children in care

No. of deaf/ partially hearing children in care	NDCS 1977 No. of LAs with this no. of 'deaf' children	NFCA 1980/81 No. of LAs with this no. of 'totally deaf' and 'hard of hearing' children	BDA Working Party 1989 No. of LAs with this no. of 'profoundly deaf' and 'partially hearing' children
1	17	12	14
2	9	10	8
3	8	4	4
4	5	2	4
5	1	2	1
6	–	2	–
7	–	–	–
8	–	1	–
9	–	1	–
	40 LAs with a total of 91 children*	34 LAs with a total of 91 children**	35 LAs with a total of 70 children***

Notes

*7 local authorities in the NDCS survey reported having deaf children in care but did not specify the number.

** 21 local authorities responding to NFCA either did not know or did not specify how many 'totally deaf' or 'hard of hearing' children were in their care.

*** Responses to the BDA working party questionnaire included 34 nil returns from local authorities.

Table 2

Deaf children with additional disabilities

Total no. of profoundly deaf children in care	No. with additional disabilities	Total no. of partially hearing children in care	No. with additional disabilities
36	12	34	14

Table 3

Ethnic origin

	Total	No. with additional disabilities
	Partially hearing and profoundly deaf	Partially hearing and profoundly deaf
Black (incl. African, Caribbean and Asian)	10	3
Other ethnic minority	–	–
White	60	23

Twenty-four children were in children's homes, residential schools for 52 weeks a year, or in hospital. Ten of these children had additional disabilities, and only six were recorded as waiting for adoptive families.

Forty-four children were with foster families, prospective adopters or relatives. Sixteen of these children had additional disabilities and five were awaiting foster or adoptive families. (See Table 4.) Given the relatively small number of deaf children in care and the limited response to the questionnaire, we are not able to draw firm conclusions about the influence of additional disabilities on current placements.

Table 4

Placements (PH = partially hearing PD = profoundly deaf)

	Total		No. with additional disabilities	
	PH	PD	PH	PD
With relatives	4	5	2	1
With foster parents – long term	11	15	5	6
– short term	4	1	–	–
With prospective adoptive family	2	2	1	1
In children's home	10	8	5	1
In residential school – 52 weeks a year	1	4	1	2
In hospital	–	1	–	1
Elsewhere	2	–	–	–
	34	36	14	12

In 1987/88, as part of a separate consultation exercise, we contacted 62 schools for deaf and hearing-impaired children about their experience of substitute care. Thirty-eight of them provided information about children they knew to be in care.

Sixty-five children attending 29 of the 38 schools were known to be in care. Almost three quarters of them (48) were attending schools with residential provision and a high proportion (43) had additional needs arising from physical and/or mental disability or other difficulties. Twenty of the children were in residential care (14 of whom had additional special needs), 37 were with foster families (23 with additional special needs) and eight were with their own families (six with additional special needs). Most of the children with additional special needs (36) were in schools with residential provision, whilst only seven of the 17 day school pupils had additional special needs.

The experience of care

The NDCS survey, our enquiries to schools, consultations with deaf and hearing adoptive and foster parents, professional child care workers and the wider Deaf Community all provided an invaluable source of experience and comment on many of the issues involved in the care of deaf children. In addition, we noted that many of the concerns and questions raised in our deliberations had received attention in the USA through the work of Advocates for Hearing Impaired Youth, Inc. (AHIY), an organisation established in 1982 '. . . for the purpose of assessing the needs of the estimated 4,000 to 5,000 children with hearing impairments placed under the care of social services agencies [and] committed to providing child placement professionals with some awareness and sensitivity to these special needs. The effort has grown out of the perception that in most cases deaf children are inappropriately placed in substitute care.'[3] Although comparisons with the situation in other countries need to be approached with caution, we refer below to AHIY's experience.

Consistency of care placements

In our enquiries to schools we asked teachers whether they had concerns about the availability and/or consistency of care/placements (for example, during holiday periods for children in residential schools). A quarter of the respondents expressed concern and it was interesting to note that virtually all those who commented on this question referred to placements in residential homes. They mentioned the need for consistency in communication, and the importance of carers being able to continue and reinforce methods used in school. There were comments about children regressing considerably during school holidays and about behaviour problems re-emerging. Turn-over in staff and poor staffing ratios in residential placements were thought to be part of the cause, but the main reason given was lack of communication skills in the children's residential environments. A social worker who wrote to the working party took the same view: 'Recently two student social workers working in residential care in different areas of the country were asked to care for two deaf children. The children were at residential school and the home provision was in lieu of suitable foster care being available. The students told me of their concern that no one at the residential home could communicate well with the children.'

The resources for deaf children who need short term care are inadequate and some schools experienced difficulty in finding suitable placements. Examples were given of deaf children needing regular periods of temporary care, families needing support and respite during holiday periods, and children from abroad needing fostering by families close to the schools.

We heard of one school for the deaf catering for deaf children with additional disabilities where care is provided for 52 weeks of the year, but this is unusual and some children can be placed in inadequate hospital or residential placements during holidays. As one school commented, 'this undoes a lot of good learning'. Foster/adoptive homes suited to the needs of profoundly deaf children are in short supply. To quote another school: 'At a traumatic time, children are placed with families who are unable to communicate.' AHIY has also expressed concern that: 'Because of family crises, placements frequently occur without much time for planning. The deaf child is often placed with foster families who have boundless goodwill but no knowledge of the disability and no Sign Language skills.'

Finding suitable foster/adoptive families
The experience of AHIY raises questions about the reasonableness of expecting even experienced substitute families to meet the particular needs of a deaf (and probably multiply disabled) child and to acquire the vital communication skills. Like many of those we consulted, AHIY concludes that it is essential to identify foster families who understand deafness and already have communication skills.

Although eight local authorities replying to the 1977 NDCS survey did not see the need for foster parents to have 'any special training or experience in caring for a deaf child', the majority acknowledged the need for families with experience of this task. Awareness of the need, however, did not lead to recruitment of such families. Most agencies apparently used experienced foster parents of hearing children and gave them varying degrees of support in facing 'the additional problems posed by deafness'; a few mentioned the use of deaf adults, staff of schools for the deaf and parents of deaf children as potential carers.

In the NFCA survey only three agencies indicated that they would seek advice from specialist workers with the deaf, and two stressed that the ability of foster parents to communicate with the deaf or hard of hearing child was more important than whether they were themselves deaf. This view was neatly expressed by one NDCS respondent: 'No matter how well suited a person might be, unless there is full and early communication between foster parent and child the whole scheme is likely to create more problems than it solves.'

A decade later we found that foster/adoptive parents of deaf children still appear to be chosen not because they possess any particular knowledge or experience of deafness, but because they are available. For example: 'The B family's fostering occurred purely by chance in that they met Rachel through social contact with a friend who worked at the establishment where Rachel had lived for several years.' Another foster mother reported that the family 'had received no specialist support from the social services department and had not known where Sign Language tuition could be arranged'. Eventually she discovered for herself that such provision was available and the local authority paid for the classes, but she had to suggest this herself. Our survey also revealed that deaf parents are still a much under-used resource – only one deaf child was placed with one or more partially hearing or deaf foster/adoptive parent.

The fact that there are only a relatively small number of deaf children in care and only a few in the care of any one authority only partly explains a lack of knowledge and experience of the particular needs of deaf children amongst child care workers. In our consultations we found other contributory factors, including the under-use of specialist social workers with deaf people as co-workers, the low level of public awareness of the Deaf Community (and the potential resource it represents), and deaf people's own limited knowledge of the need for substitute families.

In our correspondence and discussions with schools, families and fostering/adoption workers it was evident that these factors also affected substitute families' access to information and guidance on caring for a deaf child. The experience of two families was typical:

> Only gradually had the family understood what the implications of having a deaf child were. Foster parents need a lot of support and Christine and her husband did not get it – it was they who had to find the help themselves.

> Post-placement support was minimal. No guidance has been offered on deafness and it was clear that such support and help as

the family had been able to acquire was solely through their own efforts.

Comments from over three quarters of the schools criticised the levels of support presently offered to foster/adoptive parents. As one respondent put it: 'Problems have arisen due to inappropriate and ineffectual advice. Social services fostering and adoption staff appear to have no knowledge of profound, prelingual deafness . . . '

Where social workers lack the ability to explain or discuss with deaf children the plans and decisions made about their lives, then, as AHIY found, the result will be: 'Frustration and disappointment for family and child. The child faces two alternatives: quiet "adjustment" to a setting that affords very limited communication and often results in a sense of isolation that is extremely damaging, or acting out behaviour that precipitates one move after another.'

Schools reinforced the view that it was essential to find suitable carers with skills in communication, particularly BSL, and to provide information, training and ongoing support for them. Information-sharing and liaison among agencies involved with deaf children was felt by some to be less than adequate. A number of schools stressed the importance of an effective network linking the family, school and agency as a means of providing advice and information to families and agencies and of ensuring consistency and continuity in the care and education of the children. They also expressed specific concerns about a lack of understanding of the way difficult behaviour was exacerbated by an inability to communicate and of the fact that children who have suffered separation or trauma will experience greater emotional upheaval if they are unable to express themselves freely, be understood or understand their carers. The consequent additional stress on both child and carers only increased the risk of rejection and breakdown of the placement.

These responses from the schools underline the necessity for both the agency and substitute family to be properly prepared for the task of meeting the needs of a child who has to deal with earlier confusion or damaging experiences within the constraints and frustrations imposed by communication problems and, in many cases, additional handicaps.

Support services for families who foster/adopt deaf children

Support for families providing substitute care for deaf children must allow for individuality – no two families are the same, and sensitivity has to be shown to the needs, wishes and capabilities of the carers. Nevertheless we can identify areas of common need. These needs should be met not by individual professionals working in an isolated, unconnected way, but by a coherent team approach. This should be based on multi-disciplinary co-operation and assessment, incorporating planned social work input and the appropriate use of voluntary sector services and the Deaf Community.

Possible sources of professional support for the carers of a deaf child are numerous and may include the following:

Medical: Ear, nose and throat (ENT) consultant/surgeon: paediatrician; audiological physician; health visitor; speech therapist.

Educational: peripatetic teacher of the deaf; educational psychologist; teacher of the deaf at a school; educational audiologist.

Social work: social worker; specialist social worker with deaf people.

Voluntary: organisations of and for deaf people (see Appendix III): informal networks of the Deaf Community.

The focus for multi-professional assessment and planning can vary. At the stage of diagnosis, hospital children's centres play a significant role. Later on, assessment for special educational needs under the 1981 Education Act becomes significant (see Chapter 4). At any age a social services focus will be provided by reviews of a child in care or case conferences. Whatever the focus, prospective foster/adoptive parents need to be considered as key workers, sharing as fully as possible in the consultation and planning process for the child and receiving the training and resources they require.

A multi-professional approach is built into the parent guidance courses provided by the Ealing Family Centre, London, under the auspices of the Royal Eye, Nose, Throat and Ear Hospital. The consultant ENT surgeon in the family's home area can make the referral to the centre. It acts as a national resource providing four-day courses which are built around a multi-disciplinary assessment of the child, and tailored to the needs of the particular child and family attending. The whole family unit is encouraged to attend wherever possible, and the importance of interaction within the family is recognised. The centre gives parents an opportunity to raise problems they may be experiencing with their deaf child and provides appropriate advice, information and counselling. A similar service for deaf-blind children provided by SENSE Family Advisory Service is described in Appendix III.

Common needs of 'hearing' carers

Freeman, Carbin and Boese[4] examine the needs of parents bringing up their own deaf child. Whilst some of their analysis is applicable only to birth parents, many of the issues they raise are equally relevant to all carers, whether foster or adoptive parents. We consider these now.

Opportunities to question and learn about deafness

Foster/adoptive parents need to be prepared as early as possible with all the information they require about the implications of deafness throughout life: the acquisition of spoken and Sign Language; literacy; communication and educational skills; possible developmental and social difficulties; and how positive strategies for enabling deaf children to communicate, develop language and acquire a positive self-identity can help them develop and realise potential.

It is important to encourage hearing carers of profoundly deaf children to consider what attitude they should take towards deafness and deaf people. We found, as did AHIY, that: 'Frequently there is the subconscious hope, by both natural and foster parents, that if enough energy is invested, the deaf child will eventually become like a hearing person. However, when the disability does not magically disappear, many parents become discouraged. The reality is that the deaf child does not become like them.' The 'normality/integration' approach is still reflected in the attitudes and practice of many hearing professionals in the fields of medicine and education. They view deafness as a 'defect to be remedied'. This conflicts with the approach that seeks to achieve a mature personality and identity which accepts that 'it is all right to be deaf'. This latter approach emphasises a respect for Sign Language and Deaf culture, and views deafness as a difference to be accepted.

Most important to the family is long-term contact with reliable, knowledgeable people who respect and accept deaf people and to whom the parents can relate with confidence and trust. Social workers with special knowledge of deafness, and deaf adults in a variety of professional and voluntary roles, are important sources of information, support and reassurance.

Establishing rewarding communication between child and family
Good communication is vital in establishing relationships but, as we have seen, there is little evidence that carers of deaf children are receiving special assistance.

Increasingly schools and units for deaf children are following a Total Communication approach (which includes the use of Sign) as are peripatetic services for pre-school children. There is increasing provision for parents to acquire Sign Language skills but it tends to be more accessible to those living close to schools or urban centres. Agencies should explore specialist sources to ensure that early and consistent communication training for substitute families is available. This should involve at a minimum: individual tuition and support, preferably from a trained Sign Language tutor, and provision of relevant materials such as books, videos, etc; and a support programme which should seek to involve the whole family and avoid a situation where mainly the mother assumes responsibility. Other relatives and interested parties like neighbours, friends and local hearing children should be included wherever possible; in the case of pre-school children, nursery or play-group staff should be drawn in to ensure a full communicating environment for the child. Where possible parents should be put in touch with parents' courses or other Sign Language courses/groups to enable them to develop ability to stimulate the child; they should not be left to lag behind and then have to catch up. They should not have to do this at extra cost to themselves in course fees, travel costs, etc.

The involvement of Deaf adults serving as a language and role model for the deaf child and for the foster/adoptive parents will help communication. The child sees 'someone like me', a Deaf person who is a significant figure in his/her life, and learns to feel positively about Deaf identity. This would help to prevent the sort of unhappy situation described by one foster parent: 'Alan had no communication skills, any more than Jean and her husband. He thought that as he grew older he would hear.'

Practical support
'She has been told that fostering a deaf child does not involve any enhanced rate to foster parents. Enhanced rates were only for children with serious handicaps . . .'

Responses such as this to one of the foster mothers we met fail to recognise that caring for deaf children who may have behaviour difficulties, either through emotional disturbance, frustrated communication or additional disability like rubella damage, can be highly stressful, time-consuming and expensive. Tantruming may impose heavy wear and tear on the home. Young deaf children need extra supervision and attention, sometimes because of the greater difficulty in settling a deaf child at night, or the difficulties in explaining and avoiding dangers from external hazards like traffic, and domestic hazards like electric sockets. These factors should be reflected in adequate and enhanced fostering allowances.

Parents and carers of deaf children need information about state benefits such as attendance allowance and grants from voluntary sources like the Family Fund. Carers may be refused these benefits and need advice and assistance in order to appeal. They may experience practical difficulties in gaining admission to suitable play-group or holiday play schemes. A social worker knowledgeable about deafness or specialist voluntary organisations can identify resources and provide advocacy for carers facing such obstacles.

The potential usefulness of practical aids and equipment such as visual baby alarms and deaf communicating terminals (DCTs) need to be explored with carers. These environmental aids are available from social services departments under the provisions of the 1970 Chronically Sick and Disabled Persons Act.

Backup/respite care
Flexible relief/respite care in a communicating environment can help sustain the carer and thereby reduce the risk of placement breakdown. Equally, it can minimise adverse long-term effects when sudden difficulties arise, such as the illness of a carer.

Such arrangements could be of particular value where the child may have additional difficulties, such as physical or mental disabilities. One Deaf foster parent has described how another local Deaf person was recruited to act as an assistant foster mother to provide respite care, and this is an example that could usefully be followed in other areas.

Extended support post-18
Young people from the age of 18 onwards face considerable difficulties of adjustment post-school and post-care, particularly if they have

mainly experienced residential/institutional care rather than family care in their lives. These difficulties can be aggravated where the youngster is profoundly deaf. Because deafness can lead to problems of delayed maturity during adolescence, young people may experience a much longer period of transition to adulthood, and may require sensitive support. The normal process of leaving home may need to be delayed to allow for these factors. Some local authorities provide special programmes of financial and social worker support geared to assisting young people achieve independence post-18, and these should be made more widely available. Similarly, mature Deaf adults can act as role models and offer personal/family support for young deaf people to ease their access to the wider network of the Deaf Community.

Attitudes towards deaf people as adoptive/foster parents

It was clear to the working party that deaf people face formidable barriers not faced by hearing applicants when they seek to become adoptive/foster parents. When we consulted a group of Deaf people in Manchester we found that two applicants were certain they had been refused on the grounds of their deafness, and two others had heard nothing further following an initial interview. Others told us that their experience had been that deafness closes the door, that they had met with a definite 'no' and that the agencies did not want 'disabled' people.

It was widely felt that deaf people often failed to get on to the first rung of the ladder of acceptance because of the perception of them primarily as disabled and, therefore, inadequate individuals. As AHIY put it, 'When deaf adults are seen in this light, they are perceived as those who receive services rather than as possible providers. Often, child placement agencies do not see the Deaf Community as having capable adults who can impart valuable coping skills to deaf youngsters.' These attitudes are manifested not only by fostering/adoption social workers, but, equally importantly, by members of decision-making committees in local authorities and by professionals in other fields, such as audiological services. As one social worker reported: 'Unfortunately the idea that deaf people are considered to be unfit [for fostering/adoption] has strong roots in the social services set-up.' Regrettably, these perceptions of deaf people underestimate or deny the potential contribution of deaf individuals as carers. They also fail to grasp the advantages that deaf people can enjoy in the care and upbringing of deaf children. Deaf people often develop their interest in adoption and fostering informally through chance encounters with other people who have become active in fostering or adoption. Our consultations showed that there was considerable confusion and lack of understanding (as amongst many hearing people) about basic issues, such as the difference between fostering and adoption; how long it took to be approved; and whether deaf people could foster/adopt non-disabled children.

The experience of rejection and struggle by deaf applicants was not a universal one, however. There is some evidence to suggest that where progress was made by deaf applicants there had been help from an intermediary or advocate. For example, in one case a social worker with deaf people had to do a great deal of ground-work, including arranging meetings between members of the fostering and adoption panel and the Deaf applicants, before approval was finally given for the family to foster deaf children and hearing children of deaf parents. In another case the support of a local clergyman had initially proved helpful to the couple who applied. It seems that deaf people who wish to foster/adopt need to be assertive, determined and persistent in order to succeed.

There appears to have been little change in the attitudes of fostering/adoption agencies towards deaf people as potential substitute parents in the few years since the NFCA survey. In reply to a broad question asking whether applications would be discounted if one or both parents were 'deaf' or 'hard of hearing', only four of 59 NFCA respondents said they would discount 'deaf' applicants, and none would discount 'hard of hearing' applicants. However, a more detailed profile of prevailing prejudices emerged from specific questions which differentiated between 'totally deaf' and 'hard of hearing' applicants and single parents in both these groups. Twenty-two out of 53 local authorities stated that they would not consider applications where both parents were totally deaf. The response was similar in relation to totally deaf single parents, with 21 of 52 local authorities unwilling to consider applications. Two of 55 respondents would not accept applicants where one was totally deaf. By contrast, where both parents were hard of hearing only four would refuse to consider applications and only two would refuse in the case of a single hard-of-hearing parent. None of the local authorities said they would discriminate if one of the two parents was hard of hearing.

Finally, NFCA asked what the reaction would be to applicants and the placement of hearing-impaired and 'other children' where one parent was deaf and the other hard of hearing. Seven of 51 replied that they would not consider such applications; 16 out of 55 would place only a deaf or hard-of-hearing child; and 12 out of 53 would place other children with such parents.

Because of the limited range of its questions, the NFCA survey does not support a detailed analysis of the attitudes of local authorities toward deaf and hard-of-hearing people. However, the responses support the view put to us that many local authorities either do not understand or undervalue the contribution deaf people might make in the care of deaf children.

Conclusion
The adult Deaf Community is increasingly identifying its own strengths and responsibilities towards deaf children and their families. It is recognising its capacity to offer families the benefit of individual and collective experience, skills in communication and role models for deaf children. Equally important for parents is the ability of Deaf people to address and dispel many of the misconceptions surrounding Deaf adulthood, Sign Language and Deaf culture. In later chapters we explore the sources of these strengths and their potential for meeting some of the needs of deaf children and families.

References

1 National Deaf Children's Society *Fostering survey* 1977.

2 National Foster Care Association *Fostering survey* (unpublished) 1981.

3 Acrari M and Betman B 'The deaf child in foster care' *Children Today* Vol 15 Pt 4, 1986.

4 Freeman R, Carbin C and Boese R *Can't your child hear?* Croom Helm, 1981.

3 The causes and meaning of deafness

Deaf children have needs similar to those of hearing children, but because they cannot hear well they may need to communicate in ways which are different from those of other children.

What do we mean by deaf? The word is very elastic and has come to be used in much the same way as hearing impairment. Traditionally the term deaf was solely ascribed to those individuals who were profoundly or severely deaf. Nowadays the two terms, deafness and hearing impairment, are seen in many quarters as synonymous. The National Deaf Children's Society (NDCS) uses the word 'deaf' to describe all forms of hearing loss in children, that is, from the mildest to the most profound.

Deafness, as we shall see throughout this book, may not be just a prescribed degree of hearing loss, with its attendant needs, but may also be a term to denote a certain cultural uniqueness and identity. Terms such as hearing-impaired are therefore felt by many Deaf people to be pejorative, portraying a negative image. In contrast many hard-of-hearing people would not wish to be labelled as deaf. There are good arguments for and against the various terminologies. In respect to Deaf people themselves and in accordance with the NDCS definition, the term deaf will be used here to describe children who have hearing losses right across the board, from the most mild at one end, to the most profoundly deaf at the other.

About half a million children are born in the United Kingdom every year. Of these, four in every thousand will be deaf. Three per thousand will be born with mild to severe hearing losses and one per thousand will be profoundly deaf. This means that each year, on average, some 2,000 babies are born with significant hearing losses, of whom 500 will be profoundly deaf. By school entry at five years of age, when children's hearing is screened, the number with significant hearing loss increases to around six per thousand children. This is due to the number of children born hearing who subsequently lose part or all of their hearing in those early years, for example through meningitis, measles or mumps.

The causes of deafness

Deafness may be genetic in origin, or it may result from damage which occurs before, during or after birth. In a significant number of children born deaf, however, no cause can be identified.

Pre-natal

Pre-natal causes include the various conditions which are genetic in origin, that is, they have the capacity to be transmitted from one generation to the next. It is estimated that approximately one third of all childhood hearing losses are as a result of genetic factors.

The majority of children with genetically determined deafness have inherited recessive (ie suppressed or dormant) genes from both parents. It is sometimes confusing to parents and non-medical professionals when two hearing parents produce one, or in some cases several, deaf children. The children's deafness in such cases can be explained by both parents possessing a recessive 'deaf gene'. Statistically, one would expect that only one in four of the children of such parents would be born deaf.

Some forms of deafness are part of a genetic syndrome. A syndrome is a recognised collection of various conditions usually found together. An example of this is Treacher Collins Syndrome which is a combination of conductive hearing loss and facial malformations.

Some syndromal hearing losses are not genetically transmitted so may appear in just one generation but not in others – for example, Goldhaar Syndrome, which is a combination of deafness and facial malformation. Whilst both of these two congenital syndromes are often very severe in their manifestation, one (Treacher Collins Syndrome) can be transmitted as a dominant genetic condition, whilst the other cannot. The 1950s and '60s saw a large number of children born with various combinations of hearing, visual and cardiac problems as a result of their mothers contracting rubella (German measles) during the early part of the pregnancy. Nowadays rubella plays a diminished role in congenital hearing loss. The government recently launched a campaign to immunise both boys and girls against mumps, measles and rubella.

Peri-natal

Babies are very vulnerable to their environment both during and shortly after birth. This is the peri-natal period. The delicate organs of hearing, the brain and its sensitive membranes are very susceptible to infection and changes in circulation. Some babies become deaf as a result of a difficult or prolonged labour. If the oxygen supply is significantly reduced or the blood becomes contaminated by poison-ous waste products deafness may ensue. Much depends on the degree of oxygen starvation (anoxia) or blood poisoning (septicaemia).

The baby's immune system is particularly vulnerable to infection during these first few days. One of the most serious illnesses at this or any stage of development is bacterial meningitis. This infection attacks the delicate membranes of the brain's outer tissues. Many children die, partly because of the severity of the infection, and partly because meningitis is comparatively difficult to diagnose. Occasionally children who become seriously ill at this age are given drugs of the aminoglycocide group, for example, gentamycin and streptamycin. These drugs though they may prevent the baby dying from a life-threatening illness may in turn produce permanent and profound deafening. A real moral dilemma for doctors!

Post-natal
Some children born with what is thought to be 'normal' hearing become deaf during childhood. In a study carried out by the NDCS[1] it was found that about ten per cent of such children became deaf through genetic factors. One ordinarily expects genetic factors to be manifest at birth, yet some of the children in this study did not begin to lose their hearing until around the age of 12. The study found that overall 75 per cent were deafened as a result of illness, the single biggest cause, again, being bacterial meningitis. The study found that a significant number of children became profoundly deaf as a result of accidents such as falls or burns.

Why is it important to know the cause of the deafness? It is essential that every family with a deaf child should be encouraged to pursue the search for an aetiology. The major reason for its importance is to determine whether the deafness is as a result of genetic factors. This is relevant for both the parents and for the deaf child. Genetic counselling is available free through the National Health Service, and every district health authority should employ a genetic counsellor.

Types of hearing loss
Earlier on the term 'conductive loss' was used. What does this mean

and how does it differ from the term sensori-neural loss? Appendix IV shows various parts of the hearing mechanism. Sound goes through two distinct processes before being recognised by the brain: first, as sound waves travelling through the outer and middle ear; and then as electrical impulses from the cochlea to the brain via the auditory nerve. The first part of the mechanism deals with the conduction of sound and the latter part with the perception of electrical signals. Problems with the conduction of sound waves may produce 'conductive deafness', whilst impairment of the inner ear might cause what is known as 'sensori-neural deafness'. These two forms of deafness do not describe the level of hearing loss but merely the point at which the hearing mechanism is not functioning properly.

The most common cause of conductive deafness is a childhood condition called chronic otitis media or glue ear. Essentially, this is where the middle ear becomes filled with a sticky fluid which reduces the capacity of both the ear drum and the ossicles to respond to sound. Nine out of ten children get over their glue ear without resorting to medical help. Occasionally though, the condition becomes chronic and it may be necessary to respond in the form of antibiotics or surgery. The surgery is a simple process whereby a tiny hole is made in the ear drum and a minute grommet inserted into it, thereby allowing a small passage of air to help dry out the middle ear. Sometimes ear, nose and throat (ENT) surgeons will also remove the adenoids glands.

Conductive hearing losses are rarely over 80dBs. (The term decibel will be discussed later on in this chapter.) Higher levels of loss are usually found in cases where there is an absence of the middle ear, as sometimes occurs in children with Treacher Collins Syndrome, atresia of the ears or hemi-facial microsomia. Conductive losses are often treatable by surgical means. Occasionally, minor conductive losses mask a more serious and permanent loss of a neurological nature.

Sensori-neural losses on the other hand are not treatable by surgical means, yet most children do very well with the audiological help they receive. Sensori-neural loss occurs as a result of a problem somewhere in the inner ear, from the cochlea at one end to the brain at the other. Sensori-neural losses, like conductive losses, can be congenital or acquired and vary greatly in their level of severity. Losses can be from as low as 25 dB (just below normal hearing) to having no measurable hearing whatever.

Levels of hearing loss

It might be useful at this stage to look at the different levels of hearing loss.

The graph-like diagram in Figure 1 is an 'audiogram'. An audiogram is a diagrammatic representation of a person's level of hearing as plotted across two axes, one of volume measured in decibels or dBs, and the other frequency or pitch measured in Hertz or Hz.

A simple way to understand these two measures is to look at conversational speech. Speech is usually in the frequency range of 250 Hz to 4,000 Hz and at an average volume of 60 dBs. So sounds are made up of two characteristics – volume (dBs) and frequency (Hz).

A deaf child may have a hearing loss that is volume-related, frequency-related, or both. In conversational speech, for example, a child may be able to distinguish some sounds at one frequency but not at another. Using the example in Figure 1, look at the difference in sound perception when the hearing loss is at the low frequency end, compared to the higher frequency range of conversational speech:

Statement: The boy went into the sweet shop for some sweets.

High frequency loss:
−−e −o− −e−− i−−o −−e −−o− −o− −o−e −−ee−−.

Low frequency loss:
th− b−y −−nt −nt− th− sh−p f−r s−m− sw−−ts.

The difference in understanding between these two forms of hearing loss is because speech is made up of vowels and consonants. Vowel sounds are lower frequency and consonants are higher frequency. Yet speech is unintelligible if one relies solely upon vowel sounds, as the example shows.

Identifying deafness

How is deafness in children discovered? Diagnosis still takes far longer than it needs to. Usually, the first people to suspect a hearing loss are parents. Regrettably, there are still a few professionals who see parental concerns about suspected hearing loss or poor speech and language development as evidence of parental anxiety rather than possible deafness.[2] Apart from a few exceptional hospitals which run neo-natal screening programmes, most babies are first tested around the age of eight months. Profoundly deaf children are usually

Figure 1 **Audiogram**
Adapted with kind permission from AVTS (Audio-Visual Training Services) leaflet 'Medical aspects of deafness'.

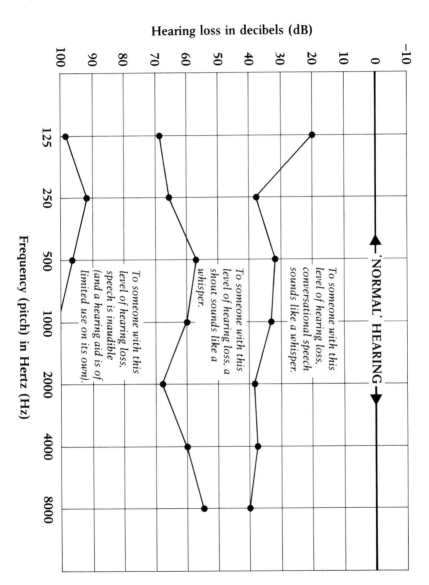

identified at the eight month screening test. Essentially, this is a simple distraction testing procedure designed to elicit a response from the baby to sound made outside of its field of vision. Unfortunately, this simple test is still often conducted in a methodologically inept manner, thus producing unrealistically high pass rates. In some district health authorities hearing screening tests are repeated throughout the early years. The children with milder hearing losses, as one would expect, are generally detected much later on, sometimes once they start school. There has been much debate about the cost-effectiveness of hearing screening, though it looks like it will stay until a more effective means is devised.

What happens after the child is suspected of having a hearing loss? Generally, children are referred to a paediatrician at the local general hospital for a complete check up, and later to either the ear, nose and throat (ENT) department or audiology clinic. In some district health authorities paediatric audiology is part of adult ENT services, and in others it is part of the general audiology services. At this stage, various tests are carried out to find out: the level/degree of hearing loss; the probable cause; and the prognosis. Medical or surgical treatment and additional help for speech and language training from a speech therapist may be required. At this stage the parents will also require help and guidance about how to handle the child's social and emotional adjustment.

Hearing aids

Once the degree of hearing loss is established, the doctors need to decide whether surgery is appropriate, as it may be for children with conductive losses, and which hearing aids if any would be suitable. If hearing aids are prescribed, these will be given free via the National Health Service. Impressions of the outer ear channel will be taken so as to produce a snug fit 'ear mould', which is the part of the hearing aid that fits into the ear. The hearing aids will be fitted on to the child and the parent told how to make best use of them.

Some hospitals and clinics do not carry a wide enough range of hearing aids to provide for a range of different skin colours. Individuals have a right to appliances whose colour tones suit their skin. Likewise, ear moulds can be clear or coloured, and where necessary are made of non-allergic materials.

It is important for parents to know where they should take the hearing aid if it breaks down or is damaged, and where to go if the tubing or mould no longer functions properly. Some hospitals encourage parents to insure their child's hearing aids. Parents do not need to insure them, and should not be charged by the hospital for losing the aids. On the other hand, some parents add the value of the hearing aids to their 'household contents' policy, and so are covered.

Cochlear implants
Sometimes misleadingly referred to as 'bionic ears', cochlear implants are a specialised form of hearing aid implanted into the child's head and embedded either within or next to the cochlea. A cochlear implant does not restore the child's hearing but does give an improved sense of sound perception. Very few children have been implanted in Britain, possibly because the group who could most benefit is very small. Implants are most suited to children who were born hearing and developed a reasonable degree of speech and language but were subsequently deafened to such a degree that they were left with no useful residual hearing. The National Deaf Children's Society has produced a package for families who are considering an implant for their child.[3]

Links with the education authority
What happens after diagnosis of deafness and the provision of hearing aids? It is difficult to generalise as the pattern varies greatly from area to area. After diagnosis, the health authority is duty bound – by section 10 of the 1981 Education Act – to do two things: first, to contact the local education authority (LEA) where the child lives informing it about the deafness; and second, to tell the parents about voluntary organisations which can provide them with support, information and advice, for example NDCS and the BDA.

In a recent report,[4] the NDCS revealed that only half of health authorities informed parents about relevant voluntary organisations, and of these helpful authorities, only about one third actually gave parents printed details about deafness and the relevant voluntary organisations.

The continuing care of the pre-school deaf child is shared between the LEA's teacher of the deaf and the paediatric audiology department. There may be other therapists and social workers who work with deaf people. Again much depends upon the area one lives in. In the next chapter we look in detail at the theory and practice of education of deaf children.

References

1 *Always a step behind* NDCS, 1987.

2 *Discovering deafness* NDCS, 1984.

3 *Cochlear implants: information for parents* NDCS, 1990.

4 *Missing link* NDCS, 1988.

4 The education of deaf children

Professionals, foster and prospective adoptive parents need to understand the educational assessment processes that deaf children will have to undergo, and to appreciate that education will be a long-term preoccupation spanning the years from pre-school to further education.

In this chapter we look at how the principal legislation on the education of children with special educational needs, the Education Act 1981, affects deaf children, their families and carers. Deaf children with multiple disabilities have additional difficulties to overcome; we emphasise that parents and professionals should have an understanding of their needs. Finally, a crucial issue in the education of deaf children is the mode of communication used and taught, and we discuss the main features of the Total Communication philosophy and the oral/aural method.

Throughout, we stress the opportunities for parental involvement in decisions about the education of deaf children – the 1981 Act's provisions include mechanisms for consultation with parents and appeal procedures at key points in the assessment process. The term 'parent' includes 'every person who has actual custody of the child or young person', so foster parents have as much right to be involved as natural or adoptive parents.

Ideally, education begins for a deaf child as soon as possible after deafness is discovered. The child's parents will also start their involvement with a learning process which will probably last as long as the child's schooling. Families need help in their search for the right sort of education for their deaf child. Parents of deaf children can often feel isolated and unsure about what to do for the best for their child. But they have one advantage – they know their child better than anyone else does. With that knowledge and a willingness to seek information and advice, they can confidently approach the professionals on more equal terms.

Diagnosis

When a child has been diagnosed as deaf, the district health authority has a duty to inform the local education authority (LEA) for the area where the family lives about the child's possible special educational needs. It should provide personal details and details about the degree of deafness and its prognosis. The LEA's chief education officer passes this information to the head of hearing-impaired services for inclusion in an assessment of the child's 'special educational needs' under the 1981 Education Act. The head of hearing-impaired services should instruct a peripatetic teacher to visit the family and offer advice and assistance, and also to begin the often lengthy assessment procedure.

The assessment of special educational needs

The special needs of a deaf child are determined by assessment often at pre-school age. The team responsible for the assessment may include an audiologist, a paediatrician, a psychologist, a teacher of the deaf, a social worker, and a speech therapist and audiological technician. The contribution of parents is a valuable resource to this team and their first-hand knowledge of the child should be used wherever and whenever necessary. Professionals often need reminding of the value of the parental contribution.

Since the 1981 Education Act decisions about where and how schooling should be arranged are no longer based on a medical model of children's disabilities. Instead, children are viewed as individuals with their own special educational needs which must be met with appropriate education. This worthy intention is not always adhered to and the 'curative' model of intervention often reappears.

The person organising all these meetings and discussions is usually 'the named officer' from the LEA described in the 1981 Act. Different members of the assessment team may take responsibility for parental guidance according to the needs involved, but in practice it is likely that it will be a peripatetic teacher of the deaf who most often visits the family. If parents are unhappy about advice they are offered or the help they receive, they can seek additional help from one of the organisations concerned with deafness, such as the National Deaf Children's Society.

If an LEA proposes to make a full assessment of a child under section 5 of the 1981 Act, it must inform the child's parents in advance. The LEA must provide information about the procedure to be followed. The parents must be supplied with the name of an officer of the LEA from whom they can get further information. The parents must also be informed of their rights to make representations and submit written evidence to the LEA, and must be given at least 29 days to do this. In the light of the contributions received, the LEA may decide not to go ahead with an assessment. Parents have a right to appeal against such a decision to the Secretary of State for Education, and the LEA must inform them of this right. If the LEA decides to go ahead and assess the child it must inform the parents, giving reasons for its decision.

Advice
Educational advice must be sought by the LEA from the head teacher of the child's school. The head must, if he or she has not personally taught the child within the preceding 18 months, consult with a teacher who has taught the child. If the child has not attended school, the LEA must call in a person with experience of teaching children with special educational needs. In cases where it is suspected that the child may be deaf or partially hearing, consultation must take place with a qualified teacher of the deaf.

Medical advice must be sought from a fully registered medical practitioner, who will be the medical officer designated for this purpose by the district health authority. This person will be responsible for co-ordinating information from all the doctors who have a contribution to make.

Psychological advice must be sought from an educational psychologist who is either employed by the LEA or engaged for the case in question by the LEA. He or she must consult with any other psychologists who have relevant knowledge or information about the child.

In addition to taking into account advice from these three sources in making an assessment, the LEA must also take into consideration any representations made, and evidence submitted, by the parents. The LEA must also consider any information that is relevant to the health or welfare of the child supplied by a district health authority or any social services department.

Examinations
The process of assessment will usually require that the child be

examined. Parents must be told in advance of any plans to conduct an examination and have a right to be present. They must be told of the time and place at which the examination will be held. The LEA must give the name of an officer from whom further information can be obtained. Parents also have the right to submit any information they wish. The right of parents to be present at examinations does not include observation of the child in a classroom over a period of time. As DES (Department of Education and Science) Circular 1/83, the guidance on assessments and statements of special educational needs, recognises, some psychological tests may need to be carried out without observers. However, the intention is to involve parents as closely as possible at all stages.

Statements
Once the assessment procedure is complete the LEA is in a position to decide whether a statement of special educational needs is necessary. LEAs do not have to make a statement on every child who is assessed. A statement is likely only to be made on a small number of children. The severely or profoundly deaf child, however, should be included in that group. The statement should include:
a) any information from the parents about the child's special educational needs, including any independent reports commissioned by them;
b) assessments of the child's special educational needs from educational, medical, psychological and any other relevant professional sources;
c) a description of the special provision the child requires including:
   (i) provision at school;
   (ii) services to be provided by the LEA;
   (iii) non-educational services to be provided by other agencies, for example, speech therapy;
   (iv) details of the proposed educational placements.
The draft statement must be sent to parents, who have fifteen days to make representations to the LEA if they disagree with the findings. They can meet with an officer of the LEA for discussion. Within a further fifteen days the parents can ask for other meetings to discuss the professional advice in the draft and within a final fifteen days from the last meeting they can make further representations to the LEA.
   The LEA after considering the parents' views can then either make

the same statement, change the draft, or decide not to make a statement at all. If a statement is made it must be sent to the parents who must be told of their right to appeal and the name of the person in the LEA to whom they can go for advice and information. If the parents are still not satisfied they can appeal in writing to the local appeal committee which can confirm the statement or ask the LEA to reconsider it. If the parents are not satisfied with the outcome of this appeal they have the right to appeal to the Secretary of State for Education.

Statements on children with special educational needs must be reviewed every 12 months. Parents should be informed of the review and be given the opportunity to discuss their child's progress. They do not, however, have the right to be present at the review. Children with statements must be re-assessed between the ages of 12½ and 14½ and the LEA must see that the special educational provision set out in the statement is carried out. However, parents can request a re-assessment at any other time if they feel there has been 'a significant change in circumstances'.

Communication

Before describing the various educational placements available to deaf children, it is appropriate to consider the approaches to communication that are currently used in their education. There are two conflicting but popular approaches: the Total Communication philosophy and the oral/aural method.

The Total Communication philosophy

The British Deaf Association defines Total Communication thus: 'the flexible use, from the earliest possible age, of a number of different communication modes (used singly or in combination) in a variety of settings.'[1] Users of Total Communication may select from the following modes:

1. *British Sign Language:* The Sign Language indigenous to the Deaf Community of Britain. It has been defined as a visual-gestural language in terms of both its perception and production. It is produced in a medium perceived visually, using gestures of the hands and the rest of the body including the face. BSL is an independent language with a structure and grammar different from that of English.

2. *Signed English:* a sign system in which the signs of British Sign Language are presented in strict English word order, with the addition of visual markers, as appropriate, to depict English grammatical constructions.

3. *Signs supporting English:* a manual support system incorporating signs taken from British Sign Language together with finger-spelling and used in English language word order to supplement speech. It is used by many bilingual Deaf people for both communication and educational purposes.

4. *British Two-Handed Finger-Spelling Alphabet:* the letters of the English alphabet transmitted manually.

5. The use of residual hearing through the amplification of sound.

6. Speech.

7. Lip-reading.

8. Reading and writing.

9. Mime and gesture.

Schools for deaf children and units for the hearing-impaired which implement this philosophy believe that in order to achieve a full education for the deaf child every available channel of communication should be used.

The oral/aural method

The aim of schools and units which use this approach is to make deaf children as similar as possible to their hearing peers, and they organise their education to that end. They argue that since deaf children will grow up to live and work in a 'hearing world', they should be taught by the same language mode as hearing children, that is, spoken language, using amplified sound and lip-reading. They believe that use of Sign Language will hinder the deaf child's use of speech and understanding of lip-reading and also that deaf children who sign tend to congregate together in a 'deaf ghetto'. So, while Total Communication accepts, and to some extent uses, the Sign Language of adult Deaf people as an educational tool to achieve access to the school curriculum for deaf pupils, the oral/aural approach makes spoken English the priority in the curriculum for the deaf child and teaches all other subjects through that medium.

There are schools for deaf children, and units for the hearing-impaired, which implement the Total Communication philosophy and others which follow the oral/aural approach.

Pre-school education

Pre-school provision is not mandatory, and is at the discretion of LEAs. Deaf children between the ages of three and five may be placed in a nursery school or class along with their hearing peers. They may be visited by a peripatetic teacher who will advise the nursery staff about their management and make sure that the children have appropriate and functioning hearing aids. In some cases the peripatetic teacher will continue to give support to the child's family, often making regular visits to the home.

The aim of this type of placement is to give the deaf child the chance to develop spoken language skills through playing with hearing children of the same age and sharing their experiences and activities in nursery education. Recently, arrangements have occasionally been made for a deaf child to attend a local nursery with the help of a Deaf adult who can explain the various activities using Sign Language. This way the deaf child is part of the larger group but has the benefit of easy, understandable communication with the Deaf adult helper. More commonly, a deaf child may attend a unit for the hearing-impaired attached to a hearing school, and is thus integrated some of the time with hearing children. Alternatively, a child may enter a nursery class in a school for deaf children where hearing pupils may be admitted or exchange visits arranged with a local nursery for hearing children. So in a variety of ways integration between deaf and hearing nursery age children may be organised.

The type of nursery placement finally agreed for a deaf child will depend on a number of factors. For instance:–
— How severe is the hearing loss?
— Where do the family live?
— Is there a nursery unit for the hearing-impaired close by?
— Is there a school for the deaf with a nursery class near the child's home?
— How does the family feel about residential education for a nursery age child?
— What is the LEA's policy on integration?

The school years

Having overcome the hurdles of the statement process and hopefully seen their child settled into the most appropriate educational provision, parents may feel that the rest is up to the professionals.

Schools for deaf children and units for the hearing-impaired which implement the Total Communication philosophy believe that in order to achieve a full education for the deaf child every available channel of communication should be used.

Photos © Linda Whitwam, photojournalist
(7 Nunroyd Road, Leeds LS17 6PH)

However, there will frequently be times when matters arise which need discussion between teachers and parents. Parents have a right to be involved in their child's education and they should always feel that they can approach their child's class teachers, advisory teachers for the hearing-impaired and other relevant educational personnel. Advisory teachers are often based at the local education office and, by liaising with the child's teacher or head teacher on the parents' behalf, they can be an additional resource for parents when their child enters school.

Parents should bear in mind when they move home that educational policies and provision may be very different in their new area from those of the area they have left. For example, some only approve of the oral/aural approach. Some children will be re-statemented when they get to a new LEA area and it would be wise for parents to investigate educational policies before deciding to move from one county or district to another. The National Deaf Children's Society should be able to give parents more information on this (see Appendix III).

Schools which are models of good practice make sure that the parents of deaf children are informed about and involved in their child's education, at the very least in the annual review and re-assessment. As we have seen, the 1981 Act has made re-assessment obligatory, though not all LEAs are implementing this part of the Act. However, most children will be re-assessed in their senior school years.

Further education
Provision of further education facilities for deaf students varies greatly within the UK. Centres do exist which provide a range of courses for students with different aptitudes and interests and some local authorities will grant financial support to young deaf people who wish to pursue these courses on a residential basis. Other authorities, however, feel that if a local FE college makes some provision for deaf students then their obligation is fulfilled and the students are expected to conform to what is provided.

FE provision should be wide-ranging to meet the various needs of deaf adolescents. For example, some deaf students may require a specialist foundation-type course in literacy, numeracy, and life and social skills. Others will cope in mainstream FE courses with support from interpreters, notetakers and both specialist and non-specialist tutors; and many will require only minimal advice and counselling to enable them to complete their course successfully. Where an LEA is unable to provide facilities in further education for a deaf student, that student's right to attend a further education course in another education authority should be recognised and financed by the student's home authority.

Multiply-disabled deaf children

The multiply-disabled deaf child is different from other deaf children in that there are extra issues to be contended with. These extra difficulties will affect the way the child is able to function; the techniques used with partially hearing or deaf children may not be appropriate.

Many multiply-disabled deaf children may not be able to function well as part of a group. They will rely on active intervention from an adult for far longer than the deaf child with no other disabilities. The child may have one or more impairments, such as visual impairment, physical disability, epilepsy, mild, moderate or severe learning difficulties and, occasionally, a related behavioural pattern. Some of these children will have a definite diagnosis, such as congenital rubella syndrome, but the disabilities of many others will not have a specific known cause. Some older children will become visually impaired in later life because of an inherited condition called Usher Syndrome. These children will have entirely different problems from other older children because they will have to adjust to the loss of sight which they have relied on in their early years.

Some multiply-disabled children may have 'glue ear' which may go unrecognised, as may the eye condition retinitis pigmentosa which affects children with Usher Syndrome.

Because of the complex nature of the whole process of diagnosis, the problems of many multiply-disabled children may be exacerbated because their other disabilities may go unrecognised. Some of these children will be under-functioning and may appear to have severe learning difficulties, or they may develop additional behavioural problems because no-one has understood the complexity of their needs. Some children may become extremely withdrawn. Some will seek attention in a variety of different ways.

The needs of deaf children with additional disabilities should be assessed very carefully. The assessment procedure should take place over an extended period of time and in all of the child's natural settings. Many multiply-disabled deaf children may not have been assessed as 'whole children' because different specialists will have concentrated on their one area of expertise.

There are specialist schools which cater for multiply-disabled deaf children throughout Britain. Many of these schools support the child as a member of the family, giving parents advice and counselling and offering support to professionals working with the child. Unfortunately, many parents of multiply-disabled deaf children will not receive the degree of practical support and guidance they feel they need and will as a result have little idea of how to communicate with their child.

Communication with multiply-disabled deaf children will be affected by their physical and visual abilities as well as their intellectual level, and sometimes the 'hands-on' or co-active signing method will have to be used. Adults working with the children will show them how to form the sign which they wish them to use. With deaf-blind children, they will be using this method to demonstrate physically what the children are required to do. Co-active signing is a special method of encouraging two-way communication between child and adult. The sensitive use of co-active signing should enable multiply-disabled children to learn the pleasure of close communication and understanding; its insensitive use may hinder their freedom to express themselves.

The psychological needs of multiply-disabled deaf children may not be appreciated by most of the professionals whom they meet. Many parents report greater difficulties in their children's teenage years than those found in able-bodied children. Some conditions are progressive, for example some young adults will have deteriorating sight and hearing; many of the physically disabled children may have persistent contraction and rigidity in the muscles or joints in later life; and young people with Usher Syndrome may be in the process of losing their most valued sense, the sense of sight. The late onset of the eye condition associated with Usher Syndrome will lead to an entirely different lifestyle with consequences that can prove devastating to them and their families.

In planning to meet the needs of multiply-disabled deaf children, very careful assessment of their separate skill areas should be carried out. Gross motor development, fine motor development, visual skills, perceptual development, social skills, hearing and communication level, daily living skills and cognitive development should all be assessed in the form of a continuous whole child programme. Emerging and developing skills will be as important to parents and teachers as the child's medical condition. The multiply-disabled deaf child has very complex difficulties and no single child will have the same needs as any other child. Children may have the same diagnosis in medical terms but their individual programme requirements may be quite different. Some children with cerebral palsy may have associated perceptual problems and even more severe communication difficulties because of their physical disability. Adaptations to take account of their communication needs will be vital.

References

1 British Deaf Association *BDA Education Policy* BDA, 1984.

5 Meeting the needs of deaf children – the contribution of deaf parents

What difference does it make for a deaf child to have deaf parents? For many years now, those working with deaf children have been suggesting that those with deaf parents have advantages in terms of their social and emotional development as well as their academic attainment and the development of their ability to communicate.

It is, however, a difficult area in which to carry out research, as will be seen in this chapter. Because of the complexity of the situation, and the number of different factors which operate, direct comparisons between deaf children of deaf parents and deaf children of hearing parents can be difficult to make. Despite this, however, there is an increasing body of evidence to suggest that for the deaf child there are positive consequences of growing up in a family where the parents are also deaf.

This chapter attempts to discuss, in as straightforward a manner as possible, the research into deaf children with deaf parents. It will look at the findings of relevant research studies, the possible reasons for such results and the implications of this work for those concerned in making decisions about the placement of deaf children.

Research into the area of deaf children of deaf parents has fallen into two distinct stages. In the 1960s and the 1970s most work concentrated on establishing what the differences were between deaf children of deaf parents and deaf children of hearing parents. More recently researchers have tried to establish how these differences came about and what could be the reason for them.

The early work

Language and communication
Language and communication is always a major issue in the consideration of the development of deaf children. This is because one of the major manifestations of deafness is difficulty in developing spoken language, and speech that is not easily understood.

This is the case at all ages. In interviews with parents of deaf pre-school children, Gregory (1976)[1] found that 76 per cent of the parents saw communication with their children as their major problem. A study of deaf school leavers showed that 48 per cent of them left school with speech that was seen as very hard to understand or effectively unintelligible. This increased to 74 per cent of those who were severely or profoundly deaf, with hearing losses in excess of 90 decibels.[2]

However studies in the early 1960s, which compared deaf children of deaf parents with those of hearing parents, showed those with the deaf parents to be at an advantage in their language development. The classic study of Stuckless and Birch (1966)[3] demonstrated that they were better on measures of speech intelligibility, lip-reading and written language. Many other studies in the 1960s had similar results, although the findings on speech intelligibility were equivocal, as not all research found differences between the two groups. Even so it should be noted that, in general, the research did not suggest that the speech of deaf children of deaf parents was less intelligible than that of those of hearing parents.

In the 1970s, work focused more on the acquisition of language by deaf children. It has long been recognised that, for the majority of deaf children, early spoken language development is slow. The study by Gregory (1976)[4] showed that 40 per cent of deaf four-year-olds and 15 per cent of deaf five-year-olds were only able to say five words or less. The same study showed that 19 per cent of four-year-olds and 17 per cent of five-year-olds could not understand anyone other than their mother. In the four-year-old group a further 14 per cent could not understand anybody at all.

Yet deaf children of deaf parents learning Sign Language as their first language did not seem to have the same problem and did not show delay in language development. The original impetus for research work on this topic was not so much the comparison between deaf children of deaf and hearing parents but a burgeoning interest in Sign Language. Work by linguists in the early 1970s was establishing the status of sign languages as true languages, and investigators became interested in how Sign Language develops in children acquiring it as their first language. An obvious group to look at here was deaf children of deaf parents.

Some of the early studies suggested that the very early linguistic development of deaf children of deaf parents was superior even to that of hearing children of hearing parents. First signs seemed to be used by deaf children at an earlier age than first words were used by hearing children.

An important stage in language development, the combination of words and signs, seemed also to emerge earlier in deaf children acquiring Sign Language than in hearing children acquiring spoken language. Schlesinger and Meadow (1972)[5] reported two-sign combinations at 14 months and Bonvillian, Orlansky and Novak (1983)[6] at 17 months. This compares with an average age for two-word combinations of about 18 months in hearing children, although the age at which children reach various milestones of language development varies considerably.

However, the situation is probably not as simple as the results may seem to indicate. When deaf children acquire Sign Language their early gestures become incorporated into their later language and thus may count as signs. Hearing children too may use gestures, but in a study of their language development these may be disregarded. Thus the comparison between the first word and the first sign may not be a fair one.

A recent study by Volterra and Casselli (1983)[7] indicates that if gestural and spoken communication are considered together, there is little difference between the rate at which deaf children acquire Sign Language and hearing children acquire spoken language. What is certainly clear from these studies is that deaf children learning Sign Language are not at a disadvantage at this stage, when compared with hearing children acquiring spoken language. Given the importance of language and communication for all areas of development this is of great significance, for it is likely to have consequences for the general development of the child as well as academic attainment.

Academic attainment
In parallel with much of the work on the language and communication of deaf children, studies also considered their academic attainment. Part of the impetus for this research was the feeling of teachers and others working with deaf children that those with deaf parents were more successful in school than those with hearing parents.

The study by Stuckless and Birch[8] which has already been mentioned, included reading as well as the other measures of language and communication. They found differences here also in favour of deaf children of deaf parents. A study in the following year of children of secondary age (11.5 to 17 years) by Meadow (1967)[9] looked at, among other things, overall achievement, reading, and also included mathematics. Deaf children of deaf parents were ahead of those of hearing parents by 1.25 years in maths, 2.11 years in reading and 1.28 years in overall attainment.

Similar results were found in several studies over the next decade and there does seem to be general agreement that deaf children of deaf parents do show some advantage. Quigley and Kretchmer (1982)[10] in their careful and considered book *The education of deaf children* say: '... there seems little doubt that on average deaf children of deaf parents perform at a higher level on certain important educational variables than do children from the general population of deaf children of hearing parents...' They then comment on the difficulty of interpreting such findings, and these difficulties will be discussed later in the chapter.

Social and emotional development

So far this discussion has focused on academic attainment. However, there were studies in the 1970s that attempted to look at the self-esteem and social adjustment of the deaf child and to compare deaf children of deaf parents with those of hearing parents.

Schlesinger and Meadow in 1972[11] examined the self-esteem of deaf children. They developed a self-image test based on cartoon drawings to which deaf children had to attribute adjectives, either positive or negative. The study was designed so that they evaluated themselves, and then gave assessments of themselves from the point of view of significant adults in their lives. The study showed that deaf children of deaf parents had more positive scores than those of hearing parents, and that they valued themselves more highly.

In their later work, Schlesinger and Meadow (1980)[12] reviewed many of the studies of social development over a period of 40 years. Overall they conclude: 'deaf children of deaf parents have been found to be relatively more mature than the deaf children of hearing parents with whom they were compared.' Later in the same book they say: 'Self-image studies of sub-groups of deaf children have shown that deaf children of deaf parents "feel more positively about themselves than the deaf children of hearing parents with whom they were compared".'

Critical analysis

These studies carried out in the 1960s and 1970s seem to establish that deaf children of deaf parents have some advantages compared with those with hearing parents. However there have been criticisms of the methodology of some of the studies. One of these criticisms is particularly important: that the success of deaf children of deaf parents was not related to the deafness of the parents but to the fact that the children themselves constituted a different sample. It was suggested that it was not the environment provided by the deaf parents that was an important factor, but the fact that deaf children of deaf parents were less likely to have problems other than deafness which could effect their attainments. The cause of their deafness would almost always be genetic, whereas for deaf children of hearing parents there could be a number of different causes, including rubella, brain-damage associated with prematurity, and anoxia at birth, all of which could be related to problems which could contribute to poorer attainment.

However, Vernon and Koh (1970)[13] carried out a study which controlled for this. They compared deaf pupils who had deaf parents with deaf pupils who had hearing parents, where the deafness in all cases was known to be due to genetic factors. This work confirmed the findings of the earlier research in that the deaf pupils of deaf parents did better on various educational and communication tests, showing that it was not the genetic differences which accounted for the results of the other studies.

Later approaches

Recently, work in the area has accepted that there are differences between deaf children of deaf parents and those with hearing parents and has attempted to show why this should be the case. Such approaches have included detailed analysis of early mother-child communication, and an examination of the home care of deaf children.

There are of course many reasons why deaf children of deaf parents are likely to be more successful that those of hearing parents. Deaf parents may be more accepting of the deafness, and they have a basic understanding of what it is like to be deaf. The children grow up in a home where deafness is normal, where it is taken for granted. It is likely that some of the visitors to the home will also be deaf. The children may also meet deaf people outside the home, at a Deaf club for example, and thus they will see many deaf people in different roles and be provided with role models. Some deaf children in hearing families never meet adult deaf people and sometimes they do not realise that adults can be deaf. They may, in fact think that they themselves will become hearing when they grow up. A 24-year old Deaf woman commented in an interview:

> When did I realise I was deaf? When I was about nine or ten I went to a Deaf club. That was the first time I realised adults were deaf. Until then I thought only children were deaf. At first I thought everbody was deaf, then only children. Then when I saw the adults I realised some adults were deaf. I realised I would grow, I would be an adult Deaf person. (Glossed from an interview in British Sign Language from work in progress by Gregory, Bishop and Sheldon.)

The development of language and communication

One of the major conclusions from early studies has been that the superiority of deaf children of deaf parents is due to the use of Sign Language by the parents. However, there are problems with this notion. Firstly, not all deaf parents use Sign Language with their children. A recent study of deaf parents in the United Kingdom suggests that probably one-third of deaf parents may use predominantly spoken language with their children (Hartley 1988).[14] The fact that until today the vast majority of deaf children were educated by oral methods means that many deaf parents do not sign to their children either because Sign Language is not their first language, or because they have adopted the idea prevalent in their own education that oral language is superior to Sign Language and therefore wish to use it with their own children.

Recently Gregory and her associates have suggested that the competence of deaf parents is not due to their use of Sign Language but because they are better at establishing those basic communication skills which are necessary for later language development. Much recent work on language development has stressed the importance of the early months for the establishment of basic communication skills. Such things as turn-taking and the establishment of a joint focus of attention seem to be important for the later development of communication.

Gregory and Barlow (in press) [15] studied the development of deaf babies, with their mothers, during their first 12 months. They demonstrated that hearing mothers had difficulty in gaining their deaf child's attention and in establishing a joint focus of activity with him or her. There were also few social initiatives from the child, in that the child rarely looked to the mother seeming to expect communication, or offered the mother a toy, or smiled at the mother.

It could be that this situation is inevitable given the child's deafness. The mothers cannot provide a background commentary to their children's play and engage with their children in that way. Thus it may be more difficult for them to develop ways of joining in the play. Also, for communication to take place, the visual channel has to be used, and this means the children have to look away from the activity in which they are engaged for communication to take place. This would seem to be very demanding for children of this age.

However, it cannot be simply a consequence of the deafness, for deaf mothers with deaf children have no such problems and the pattern of their mutual activity shows similarities to that of hearing children with their hearing mothers. The deaf mothers can gain their children's attention, a joint focus of attention is easily established and the children make many social initiatives.

Thus, even before the first word or sign, deaf parents may be more able to establish good interaction and communication. Gregory and Barlow suggest that the comparative success of deaf children of deaf parents in later life originates from the early establishment of communication which is adapted and evolved to solve the problem of using the visual channel both for communication and for their activities. This is the establishment of a smoothly co-ordinated turn-taking framework in which both mother and child are active participants.

The home care of deaf children

Recently, Hartley has completed a study [16] looking in detail at the home care of deaf children in families where the parents are also deaf. She was able to make comparisons with the practices of hearing children of deaf parents and hearing children of hearing parents by using the studies of Gregory (1976) [17] and Newson and Newson 1968) [18], as all these studies were based on similar interview schedules. A complex picture emerged and it is only possible to indicate a few of the findings here.

Hartley found that many of the problems experienced in families where the parents were hearing and the children deaf were different for families where both parents and children were deaf. For example, many of the families interviewed by Gregory had problems in getting their children to sleep and problems with their children waking in the night. A hearing mother of a four-year-old moderately deaf girl said:

> Well that's one thing we can't solve so far, because she doesn't like going to bed early. We've tried it. She'll only go to bed when her Mum goes to bed. That might be ten o'clock or eleven o'clock sometimes. She doesn't like going to bed early. If we put her to bed she'll scream and come down.

And a hearing mother of a four-year-old profoundly deaf girl said:

> She used to wake and scream every night. It used to drive us insane. Every single night she never slept through the whole night for months and months and months. It went on until she was four. Fear, insecurity, I don't know. We didn't know – we didn't know what we were doing for the first three years.

Gregory concluded: 'The area of day-to-day care which seemed to be the real problem was that surrounding sleep and bedtime.'

In Hartley's study of deaf parents of deaf children, the overwhelming majority – 90 per cent (18 out of 20) – regarded themselves as having no problems, and, in general, they were relaxed over the whole issue of sleep and bedtime. Two of the deaf mothers described bedtimes for their children as follows:

> I take Alison upstairs, I tell her it's bedtime ... (description of bedtime routine) ... Then she gets into bed and I sit on her bed for a minute or two, having a cuddle or kisses, then I tell her it's time to go to sleep and then leave her. I shut the door. She doesn't mind complete darkness.

> I put him in his cot, take his dummy out, give him a kiss, put his dummy back, give him a kiss, tell him to go to sleep, then bye-bye, blow him a kiss and he does the same. I wave, shut the door, about two minutes later I pop my head round the door. Tony waves, I shut

the door. Five minutes later I put my head round, he's fast asleep.

In Gregory's study another area that was problematic was that of discipline and control, and many parents said how difficult it was to convey to their child what they were allowed to do and what they should not do.

The vast majority of them (90 per cent) approved of smacking and many of them felt it was their only method of getting the message across. Even if they did not approve of smacking they often felt it to be the only option as other forms of discipline did not seem possible. A hearing mother of a two-year-old moderately deaf girl said: 'Well, I don't approve of smacking her all the while but it seems the only way you can get over to her that it's wrong, you know.' And a hearing mother of a four-year-old moderately deaf girl explained:

> Well, we could never get through to her you see, that "if you don't stop you'll go to bed in a minute", so when she was younger I told her "you'll go to bed if you keep that up" and I followed my words through and put her to bed. She'd scream hysterically in the bedroom. It wasn't fair to her. I'd have to go and get her out and think "God what am I going to do, I just can't explain to the child", so bed as a punishment never meant anything.

The deaf parents had significantly more ways available to them of getting the message across. They were significantly more likely to promise rewards in advance for being good, to deprive their child of something he or she liked as a punishment, or to threaten with an authority figure such as a policeman. One deaf mother explained: 'He understands. If you're a good boy I'll bring you some sweets, he understands. If you're a good boy you say what you want and you can go out on the bicycle.' Another deaf mother commented: 'I don't say that very often, but I sometimes warn her that you won't have any sweets if you don't do this or that. I don't do it very often.'

It is not the relative merits of these different methods that is at issue here but the fact that deaf parents had a much greater range of options available to them.

The differences found in Hartley's study cannot just be due to the use of Sign Language by the deaf parents, for as she points out, not all the parents used Sign Language with their children. She feels it was the

*Deafness does not necessarily inhibit the development of language
and communication or limit academic attainment.*

*Photo © Linda Whitwam, photojournalist
(7 Nunroyd Road, Leeds LS17 6PH)*

mothers' inbuilt understanding of deafness and their sensitivity to their deaf children which was important. In her concluding chapter, she says:

> The most important fact that emerged . . . was the mother's tacit knowledge of deafness which facilitated effective interaction between parent and child and consequently influenced all aspects of child rearing . . . It may be that effective social interaction is more important in accounting for the superior academic performance of deaf children of deaf parents compared with deaf children of hearing parents than is mode of communication. Certainly, the results of this present study would support this assertion.

Implications of the research

For many professionals concerned with deaf children research studies such as these indicate the potential of deaf children. Deafness does not necessarily inhibit the development of language and communication or limit academic attainment. It is clear that much can be learnt from deaf people about the care of deaf children. As Hartley says,

> Perhaps the best that can be hoped for is that parents and professionals concerned with young deaf children will understand more about the experiences of deaf families and by coming into close contact with deaf people will assimilate some of their wisdom concerning deafness.

For those concerned with the placement of children for adoption and fostering it is clear that deaf parents may have a great deal to offer. The evidence shows that deaf parents do not inhibit the development of deaf children, and they may do a great deal to enhance it.

References

1 Gregory S *The deaf child and his family* George Allen and Unwin, 1976.

2 Conrad R *The deaf school child* Harper and Row, 1979.

3 Stuckless E and Birch J 'The influence of early manual communication on the linguistic development of deaf children' *American Annals of the Deaf* 111, 1966.

4 See 1 above.

5 Schlesinger H and Meadow K *Sound and Sign: childhood deafness and mental health* University of California Press, 1972.

6 Bonvillian J, Orlansky M and Novak L 'Early Sign Language acquisition and its relation to cognitive and motor development' in Kyle J and Woll E (eds) *Language in sign: an international perspective on Sign Language* Croom Helm, 1983.

7 Volterra V and Casselli M 'Gestures, signs and words' in Stokoe W and Volterra V (eds) *Sign Language research* Linstock Press, Instituto di Psicologia CNR, 1983.

8 See 3 above.

9 Meadow K *The effect of early manual communication and family climate on the deaf child's development* University of California Press, 1967.

10 Quigley S and Kretchmer R *The education of deaf children* Edward Arnold, 1982

11 See 5 above.

12 Meadow K *Deafness and child development* Edward Arnold, 1980.

13 Vernon M and Koh S E arly manual communication and deaf children's achievement' *American Annals of the Deaf* 115 527–536, 1970.

14 Hartley G *Aspects of the home care of deaf children of deaf parents* unpublished PhD thesis, University of Nottingham, 1988.

15 Gregory S and Barlow S (in press) 'Interaction between deaf babies and their deaf and hearing mothers' *Journal of Sign* Vol 1.

16 See 14 above.

17 See 1 above.

18 Newson J and Newson E *Four years old in an urban community* George Allen and Unwin, 1968.

6 The role of the Deaf Community in supporting deaf children

In chapter 2 we established that deaf parents have much to offer the deaf child. In this chapter we consider what the wider Deaf Community can offer. In a recent court judgment about the placement of a deaf child, much was made of whether or not the child would develop 'oral' communication and scant attention was paid to other needs of the child – the nature of deafness, the richness of Deaf culture and its support systems. The case exemplified the common attitude to deafness as solely a disability, with little or no understanding of the reality of Deaf culture and community.

Baker and Cokely[1] give two definitions of deafness. Pathological – which accepts that the behaviour and values of the hearing majority are the 'norm' and then focuses on how deaf people deviate from this 'norm'. It is an approach which seeks to 'repair' deaf people so that they may become as 'normal' as possible. Cultural – which focuses on the common language, shared experiences, etc, which characterise a particular group of people who happen to be deaf. It conceives of the Deaf Community as a separate cultural group with its own values and language. Schlesinger and Meadow[2] describe the Deaf Community as 'a group of persons who share a common means of group communication which provides the basis for group cohesion and identity'.

The Deaf Community comprises a wide variety of individuals, employed in most trades and professions, from all walks of life, in exactly the same way as does the hearing community. Deafness itself does not affect a person's intellectual capacity or ability to learn, but deaf children generally require some sort of special education. (The range of educational provision is more fully described in chapter 4.) On starting school, the deaf child begins to identify with other deaf children. They become a community bound by their common need to communicate with each other: 'Attendance at residential schools is considered one of the most formative influences in acquiring that basic Deaf identity which grants access to the Deaf Community.' (Brien[3])

In reality the Deaf Community is not limited to those who attended residential schools, influential though this group may be. Padden[4] defines the Deaf Community as 'including people who are not themselves deaf but actively support the goals of the community and work with deaf people to achieve them'. She defines culturally Deaf people as those who 'behave as deaf people do, use the language of deaf people and share the beliefs that deaf people have about themselves and about those who are not deaf', and draws attention to the different variants of Sign Language used within the community.

Deaf clubs, which are found in most large towns and cities throughout the country (and some small ones), are the mainstay of the Deaf Community and are the places where Deaf people go to relax, find companionship, usually meet marriage partners, and are able to communicate easily in their own language. Deaf people acquire a positive identity and self-esteem and, as a group, are able to exert influence on matters which directly affect them. As individuals, they live and work in a hearing world which is full of prejudice and ignorance. Deaf people are frequently under-employed and under-valued members of society but through their communities and the organisations to which they belong, they have, particularly in recent years, made great progress in remedying this state of affairs.

Young deaf people may find difficulty in learning about the wider world of work and society generally, because of communication difficulties which may exist and because of prevalent attitudes to deafness in the hearing community. However, in the Deaf Community they can find role models, counsellors, advisers and much wisdom from the older members of the community. These people can give the younger members the benefit of their knowledge, offering support at times of stress and change, helping them to become more confident, secure and optimistic and to feel that 'it's alright to be deaf'. In a community where access to written material is, to a great extent, denied, this accumulated knowledge and wisdom is invaluable. It cannot be found in the hearing world.

It is far from true that life within the Deaf Community is restricted. Although an individual deaf person in a hearing environment will be likely to be isolated, unable to communicate in a group and may even have difficulty on a one-to-one basis, these restrictions do not apply in the Deaf Community where Sign Language, being a visual mode, is accessible to all present. Groups of Deaf people, usually with an interpreter, arrange events of an educational nature, of general interest or entertainment through clubs. They participate with hearing people in local events, not least in sporting activities. In some areas they attend meetings of local councils, particularly when matters affecting them are being discussed. At national level, they are involved in campaigns to gain recognition of their needs, their rights and, especially, of British Sign Language. Overall, the Deaf Community increases the opportunities for involvement and participation of deaf people in matters which directly impinge on their individual lives. Deaf people are enabled to contribute through their community and generally live more fulfilled lives. The Deaf Community broadens the options of the young deaf person to an extent which would be denied without its existence. 'Its culture comprises a range of activities which are sufficiently powerful to nullify, for the majority of deaf people, the negative experiences of daily life.' (Brien[5])

Deaf children who, for whatever reason, are unable to live with their own family may have no idea of what is happening to them. Given a spoken vocabulary of about five words, like almost half the four-year-old children in Gregory's study (see chapter 5), how is the child care worker or foster or adoptive parent able to help the child to understand, to offer some simple explanation, to comfort and reassure the child at such a time of trauma? A Deaf adult, suitably selected, could communicate far more satisfactorily than any hearing adult. Deaf foster or adoptive parents could use their great repertoire of communication methods in caring for and nurturing a deaf child, and could ensure a wide circle of communicating Deaf 'aunts, uncles and cousins' in the Deaf Community to give the deaf child the love and security which every child needs. It is the right of every child needing a placement away from its family to be found a substitute family which best meets the need for social and emotional development. For a deaf child, this may well be with a Deaf family.

The Deaf Community now needs to be made aware of the tremendous contribution it can make to child care for deaf children. Much effort is needed to overcome the negative experiences and prejudices they have so far had to face, and which were so evident during the working party's investigations. The preparation of videos with signed interpretation explaining the children's need for families, the process of selection of foster or adoptive parents, support services etc, is urgently needed. Printed material in straightforward language, using drawings and pictures and in a more visual format than usual is also needed. Agency workers who have the responsibility for placing a deaf child must also be encouraged to make personal contact with the Deaf Community. We expect these areas to be tackled by the BDA and BAAF following publication of this book. But individuals should not wait for these initiatives if faced with the imminent prospect of placing a deaf child – the list of addresses in Appendix III will give contact points where advice and assistance should be readily available.

References

1   Baker and Cokely D *American Sign Language – a teacher's resource text on grammar and culture* Silver Springs: T J Publishers, 1980.

2   Schlesinger H and Meadow K *Sound and Sign: childhood deafness and mental health* University of California Press, 1972.

3   Brien D 'Is there a Deaf culture available to the young deaf person?' Loughborough NCSWDP Conference 1981.

4   Padden C *The deaf community and the culture of deaf people* Washington DC: NAD (quoted by David Brien).

5   See 3 above.

7   The language needs of deaf children – BSL and sign systems

In Britain today there is a growing awareness of and respect for the many different minority groups which make up our increasingly pluralistic society. However, there is one linguistic and cultural minority about which comparatively little is known – Britain's Deaf Community. There are up to 50,000 people across the United Kingdom in this minority group. Most of them have been born deaf or been deafened before acquiring mastery of spoken English, and they use as their first or preferred language BSL (British Sign Language). After English, Welsh and Gaelic, this is the fourth most commonly used language in Britain today.[1]

BSL (British Sign Language)
It is often assumed that the Sign Language of the Deaf Community is but a manual representation of English. This is far from the case. BSL is a natural, visual-gestural language which has evolved (like English) over many centuries (there are early references to Sign Language in the writings of Bulwer in 1644 and Pepys in 1666) and which has a grammar quite independent of English. The position of signs in any signed utterance are not random; they conform to precise rules governing spatial relationships indicated by location, direction, orientation and speed of movement of the hand, as well as the use of head and body movements, and even direction of eye gaze. It may be supplemented by the use of fingerspelling patterns and, as mouth movements tend to be unique to BSL, cannot easily be used in conjunction with spoken English.

Like any language, BSL has variations which are affected by geography (regional accent and dialect), the age and education of the signer, and the relative formality of the situation in which the conversation takes place. It is a totally efficient and functional language (it can express humour, anger, argument, cynicism, and describe things abstract, scientific and dramatic). In short, and particularly for those people denied a satisfactory oral/aural input, BSL makes visual commonsense! (Miles, 1988[2])

This was largely accepted in the early 19th century, when the special schools established to educate deaf children used the indigenous language of the community to teach spoken and written English, very often using Deaf people themselves and those who had grown up in Deaf families as teachers. BSL was acquired naturally from them, and from the small number (around 10 per cent) of deaf children with Deaf parents, in much the same way as hearing children naturally acquire spoken English from interaction with those around them. However, towards the end of the century, the tide of opinion began to turn: educationalists throughout Europe (possibly having little real understanding of the nature of language, and failing to grasp the need to separate language from speech) began to advocate a new approach to teaching deaf children – 'oralism'. Oralism (or the oral/aural method) focused on the need to teach deaf and hearing-impaired children how to articulate speech and fostered the use and development of lip-reading skills, even though the reliability of lip-reading was questionable, given the ambiguities of, for example, letters like 'p' and 'b' and 'm' and 'n'. Children could now be fitted with hearing aids to help make the speech signal more accessible, and, in the belief that manual methods of communication would hinder the acquisition of speech and lip-reading skills, Deaf teachers were sacked and pupils punished for using Sign Language.

Despite this, BSL did not go away, and like other repressed minority languages (for example, Gaelic and Catalan) merely went 'underground'. Deaf people were inevitably influenced by the very negative weight of opinion against Sign Language held by those in authority, who regarded it as 'inferior/concrete' and 'sub-human' (Van Uden, 1977[3]). They were led to regard it as shameful, second-class and inferior. Nonetheless, they continued to use it amongst themselves, and indeed, in 1890, the British Deaf Association (at that time the British Deaf and Dumb Association) was formed by members of the Deaf Community in an attempt to fight for the retention of Sign Language within the educational system.

Total Communication and sign systems

Educational practice in the following years was largely committed to an oral/aural approach for all deaf and hearing-impaired children. However, in the late 1960s and early '70s, there appeared to be growing dissatisfaction, not only from pupils and parents, but within the teaching profession, at the low levels of attainment reached by deaf school-children. Research carried out by Conrad between 1974 and 1976[4] confirmed these depressing levels and pointed to the tremendous difficulty inherent in learning oral language for those unable easily to perceive the spoken word. It also drew attention to the frightening lack of 'internal language' in the profoundly deaf child, and demonstrated that it was difficult for many deaf children to maximise learning through purely oral methods. Other studies in a number of countries (Schlesinger and Meadow, 1972[5]; Montgomery, 1976[6]) had shown that contrary to former belief, the use of Sign Language by young deaf children did not prove detrimental to intellectual development and the use of speech and lip-reading skills. Gradually, a philosophy known as 'Total Communication' began to be accepted. The British Deaf Association defines Total Communication as 'the flexible use from the earliest possible age of a number of communication modes (used singly or in combination) in a variety of settings'.

The original philosophy of Total Communication, initially expressed by Denton (1976)[7] was 'the right of a deaf child to use all forms of communication available to develop language competence.' It therefore includes oral/aural methods, sign systems, mime and gesture, reading and writing, and BSL. It has not been as successful for all children as might have been hoped. In practice, Total Communication meant spoken English accompanied by some manual coding of English, and this continued to deprive numbers of deaf schoolchildren easy access to language.

Educationalists, keen to meet the needs of a wide variety of deaf and hearing-impaired children and recognising the need to input information visually, began to create a number of artificial sign systems, many of which continue to be used today. These include:

Cued speech
Cued speech is a system of signals used to aid lip-reading, developed by Dr Orin Cornett in 1967. It consists of lip movements and supplementary handcues made near the face and used in conjunction with speech, which enable a speaker already familiar with the language patterns to make phonetic distinctions. There are a few schools and units for deaf and hearing-impaired children in Britain which use this

method (usually with other educational approaches).

Paget Gorman Sign System

The Paget Gorman Sign System was devised by Sir Richard Paget and developed by Dr Pierre Gorman and Lady Grace Paget in 1968 so that a systematic and simultaneous grammatical representation of spoken English could be used with speech as an aid to teaching English. Signs were invented for this purpose and were not taken from BSL. The system was initially widely adopted by schools and units, but is much less commonly used today.

Makaton

Makaton was introduced by Johnston, Cornforth and Walker in 1973, initially to work with a group of Deaf people who also had learning difficulties. It has a specially selected core vocabulary, structured in stages of increasing complexity following 'normal' language development. Core signs are taken from BSL and key words in sentences are signed with accompanying speech. It is aimed primarily at those with learning difficulties, and although it is said to be used in one or two educational establishments for deaf children it is likely to prove too limited in application for extensive use.

Signed English

Signed English uses signs from BSL and finger spelling, as well as invented 'new' signs to represent English words, functions and inflectional endings, to accompany spoken English. The assumption is that signed English is more effective in teaching written English syntax than, for example, BSL. However, studies have found that in practice it is difficult to sustain all the markers without taking an unnatural amount of time, or, when accompanied by speech, to avoid dropping markers, and that, understandably, memorising many different signs for affixes such as 'ing', 'ed', 'dom', etc may be a problem. A child, therefore, may well be presented with an incomplete visual representation of English. Signed English is fairly widely used within education, but usually abandoned outside the classroom as it is not really an efficient means of communication.

Signs supporting English or SSE

Whilst these sign systems undoubtedly helped a number of children,

The use of Deaf people themselves as teachers and role models within the classroom cannot help but have a positive effect on the self-image of any young Deaf person.

Photos © Linda Whitwam, photojournalist
(7 Nunroyd Road, Leeds LS17 6PH)

continuing difficulties led to the adoption in the classroom of yet another form of sign communication. Signs supporting English (or alternatively sign supported English), which, some argue, might be more appropriately termed pidgin sign English, is a form of communication which uses a vocabulary of BSL signs (but not with additional artificially created signs or markers), supported by finger spelling and ordered according to English, which may or may not be used with accompanying speech. It should exploit similar spatial patterning to BSL and thereby avoid the visual incongruities present in other sign systems which did not consider the production constraints of naturally developed Sign Languages. It therefore presupposes a high knowledge of and skill in BSL.

SSE is not, however, a language, but merely a form which is used when two different groups of language users meet each other halfway, as it mixes the structures of both languages without being the indigenous language of either, and is usually dominated by English.

BSL and the maintenance of the Deaf Community
Whilst the years of overt suspicion of BSL took its toll on the members of Britain's Deaf Community, so that many professed not to know it or use it when asked by those who were hearing, it clearly survived and flourished and was freely used by Deaf people amongst themselves. However, it was not until the late 1970s and early 1980s, with the advent of research into BSL in this country by linguists at the University of Bristol and Moray House College in Edinburgh[8], and the subsequent proof that BSL was indeed a rich and complex language in its own right and not a pale and ungrammatical form of English, that Deaf people began to strongly articulate long held views.

BSL had played a vital role in the maintenance of the Deaf Community, which looked on itself not as a group of people defined by a clinical/pathological definition of deafness in which hearing loss was something to be repaired and made 'normal', but as a community with a common language, shared experiences, and positive views about the worth of a Deaf identity (Baker and Cokely, 1980[9]). Unlike other minority groups, Deaf people do not form geographical or historical communities, but, regardless of educational background, they do make a conscious choice to identify with the Deaf Community and participate in community religious, social and sporting activities. The degree and onset of hearing loss may be but a minor factor in this choice. Thus, 85 to 95 per cent of Deaf people take a Deaf spouse, and 79 per cent of profoundly Deaf people are likely to be members of their local Deaf club. (Kyle and Woll, 1985[10])

Various studies (Brill, 1969[11]; Stuckless and Birch, 1966[12]; Meadow, 1967[13]) have pointed to the superior adjustment and abilities of Deaf children of Deaf parents who have grown up with a naturally acquired language – BSL. There are a range of hearing-impaired children with varying needs, some of whom may be best served by a high quality oral education and communication, but for a number a bilingual approach may be far more effective. This will mean teaching children language in the way they respond to best, using the visual gestural channel most suited to the eye (much as we would choose to concentrate on a vocal/auditory channel for those who are blind) as in BSL, and using this language, once established, to teach English as a second language, using foreign language teaching techniques.

The recent development of university courses aimed at increasing the number of trained Deaf tutors of BSL is to be welcomed as a constructive step towards facilitating the learning of BSL. Also, the work done by Ahlgren[14] in Sweden (1984) and Hansen[15] in Denmark (1986) which demonstrated that not only are parents able to acquire reasonable Sign Language skills by exposure to appropriately trained and qualified Deaf Sign Language tutors, but that deaf children themselves are well able to take in accurate Sign Language input from parents learning the language and turn it into fluent or grammatical output, should give us great encouragement to consider adopting a bilingual approach.

But, perhaps most importantly, the use of Deaf people themselves as teachers and role models within the classroom cannot help but have a positive effect on the self-image of any young Deaf person.

Experiments of this nature are occurring in some education authorities in Britain: its long-established Deaf Community awaits the outcome with considerable interest.

References

1 British Deaf Association *BSL – Britain's fourth language* BDA, 1987.

2 Miles D *British Sign Language – a beginner's guide* BBC Books, 1988.

3 Van Uden *A world of language for deaf children – Part 1 basic principles: maternal reflective method* Swets and Zeitlinger, 1977.

4 Conrad R *The deaf school child* Harper and Row, 1979.

5 See 2 above.

6 Montgomery G *Integration and disintegration of the deaf in society* Scottish Workshop for the Deaf Publications, 1981.

7 Denton D 'The philosophy of Total Communication' supplement to *The British Deaf News* August 1976.

8 Brennan M, Colville M and Lawson L *Words in hand* Moray House College, 1980.

9 Baker and Cokely D *American Sign Language – a teacher's resource text on grammar and culture* Silver Springs: T J Publishers, 1980.

10 Kyle J and Woll B *Sign Language – the study of deaf people and their language* Cambridge University Press, 1985.

11 Brill R *The superior IQs of deaf children of deaf parents* California Palms, 1969.

12 Stuckless E and Birch J 'The influence of early manual communication on the linguistic development of deaf children' *American Annals of the Deaf* 111, 1966.

13 Meadow K *The effect of early manual communication and family climate on the deaf child's development* University of California Press, 1967.

14 Ahlgren, I in lecture to Sign '84 conference. Moray House College, Edinburgh, 1984.

15 Hansen B in Trevelyan lecture, University of Durham, 1989.

8 Adoption and foster care

Previous chapters have described the experiences of deaf children and reviewed research into their needs. It is clear that a deaf child in care, in addition to the needs common to all children in care, has an all-important need for special communication skills.

As we have seen, the research from the 1960s onwards has shown that deaf children of deaf parents are at an advantage in communication skills, language development, overall educational achievement and social adjustment, when compared with deaf children of hearing parents. This could be due to a number of factors: the deaf parent's greater acceptance of deafness, more appropriate expectations of the child, greater intuitive understanding of the importance of physical contact and touch, ready access to the Deaf Community and provision of positive role models of deaf adults. Above all, deaf parents seem better able to establish good communication early in the child's life, which provides the basis from which later language develops. Also, those families where British Sign Language is the primary language of the home provide the ideal environment for deaf children to develop this language in a natural and positive way.

With this evidence before us, and in the knowledge of the importance of family life for all children, it is hard to understand the reluctance of child care agencies to recruit adoptive and foster parents from among the Deaf Community; and yet there can be no doubt that deaf adults who have offered their services have frequently met with a negative response. Some have been rejected because of their deafness, some have simply received no further communication after an initial interview and others have been told at the point of initial contact that the agency does not want 'disabled' people as foster or adoptive parents.

Since there are so few deaf children in care, it may be difficult for a child care agency to assess the level of need for families for deaf children and thus to ensure that they are available when needed. However, it should be the agency's aim and responsibility quickly to find the most appropriate family for each child in its care (whether for long- or short-term care). There must, therefore, be an obligation to provide ready access to deaf carers by ensuring that they are included in the range of families available.

A deaf child who is temporarily or permanently unable to live with his or her own family is at present likely to be in a residential school, a children's home (run by staff with little or no skill in BSL) or a hearing foster or adoptive home (see chapter 2).

Schools using Total Communication and/or providing for additional needs will not be available locally for the majority of deaf children. Thus for deaf children the unenviable choice may well be between family life and a school which meets special needs or facilitates communication and thereby individual achievement and fulfilment.

Even where children are appropriately placed in a residential school, it is crucial that they spend the holidays and, if possible, weekends with families which can meet their needs.

A residential children's home will very rarely be the placement of choice for a deaf child, who may be significantly disadvantaged and even harmed in such a setting unless the staff are deaf and/or are skilled in communicating with deaf people, and have a good knowledge of the issues surrounding deafness as well as all the other skills required of child care workers; and unless that placement in the home is for a specific purpose and aiming towards a particular goal.

Agencies are currently using hearing foster carers and adoptive families for a number of deaf children and this can be successful. However, it is important that hearing families, and in particular those without any prior experience of deafness, are properly recruited, prepared for, and supported in the task they undertake – for example, through access (at the agency's expense) to Sign Language courses and to deaf children and adults. Here, again, many child care agencies are failing their deaf children and those who care for them. Tales are common of families left to their own devices in developing communication skills, not in contact with any other carers for deaf children, and unaware of the existence of a Deaf club and Deaf Community. Other families find themselves thoroughly confused by snippets of conflicting advice from a number of different sources.

Hearing carers of deaf children need a systematic and thorough introduction to the additional needs of a child in care who is deaf. It may be possible to recruit hearing foster carers or adopters who already have some understanding and skills in this area: for example, hearing parents of a deaf child, siblings of deaf people, teachers of deaf children and hearing offspring of deaf people may all have the necessary communication skills and ready access to the Deaf Community.

Most of the requirements outlined above will, however, be most readily available in a deaf family (that is, a family in which at least one adult is deaf). It is reasonable to expect that a deaf family will have advanced communication skills, ready access to other deaf people and to the Deaf Community through clubs and so on, and a knowledge of many of the particular needs of deaf children. Such a family is in the best position to provide good role models to help the child develop a positive image.

All new families, whether deaf or hearing, experienced or inexperienced, need a reliable system of supports including ready access to consistent advice and counselling. They also need to understand how hearing loss can affect the stages of development as well as the additional factors related to the more complicated experiences of children who come into foster care. Some hearing people have expressed concern that placing deaf children with deaf families will in some way cut them off from the wider (hearing) community. This concern is unfounded. It is impossible for a deaf child to miss out on contact with hearing people since he or she is surrounded by them. Bearing in mind that virtually all nuclear families with deaf members also have hearing members and that all have hearing relatives, the risks of isolation for the child are so small as to be negligible and would, in any case, be picked up during the assessment of the family's application to adopt or foster.

The use of British Sign Language may on the surface appear to limit communication between deaf and hearing people. A judge in a recent wardship hearing addressed the question of the use of Total Communication in the education of deaf children:

> Underlying the controversy that I have touched upon, is the question whether a child should be encouraged, as far as possible, to speak and thus communicate directly with the whole of the public or whether she should seek to achieve her maximum potential, in terms of education and expression, in the more limited circle of

persons who can communicate by "Total Communication". I think that is putting the issue much too simply because there are sophisticated ramifications of it, but I sympathise with those who are reluctant to condemn a child, unless it is inescapable, to a restricted form of communication with the outside world. No-one would wish "X" to be limited to a comparatively small circle of persons who understand her, if that is avoidable.

There is a risk that this approach misses the full implications of the need for communication for every child. The choice for deaf children should not be whether to seek to belong to the hearing or the Deaf Community but whether they are offered the opportunity to belong to, participate in and benefit from the experience both communities have to offer.

Total Communication and Sign Language undoubtedly help the child to communicate more fully and thereby to achieve better and become less frustrated and more fulfilled individuals. Total Communication includes the development of speech and of lip-reading insofar as the child is able to use them and does nothing to further segregate the deaf child from the hearing society than his or her deafness has already done. It is also important to recognise that children who have forms of communication which enable them to express themselves and understand the important people around them are in a stronger position to tackle the difficulties of communication with the wider hearing community.

Recruiting deaf families

The move towards recruiting deaf families to foster or adopt deaf children in care can be tackled in a number of ways and will depend on the agency involved. Typically, agencies have either ignored the issues and turned down deaf applicants, perhaps simply through ignorance or prejudice, or they have changed their practice gradually through one or more 'test cases'. As far as we are aware, no agency yet has a policy statement of the suitability of deaf families for deaf children, although a number are working towards this.

A policy change will, of course, require a significant amount of education of people within the agency. Social workers, members of the adoption and fostering panels, senior staff and elected members or management committees may all need to be involved and the process may take a considerable time. Social workers with deaf people have an important role to play both in informing those responsible for the child care system and in acting as facilitators for deaf adults. Unfortunately, the national shortage of social workers with deaf people may mean that an agency does not have ready access to one, or that the individual's work load is too heavy for the necessary time to be available. In such cases advice should be sought from outside the agency.

It is probably more effective to proceed slowly by individual 'test cases' although this will involve a special commitment by the key workers and the family concerned. They will inevitably have to face the ignorance and prejudice which, sadly, is a facet of everyday life for deaf people, and, once again, the help of the social worker with deaf people or of other deaf people can be invaluable. In Britain, we have not moved far enough from a misunderstanding of deafness based on the argument that: 'Thinking cannot develop without language; language, in turn, cannot develop without speech; speech cannot develop without hearing. Therefore those who cannot hear cannot think.'[1]

Special publicity
The first problem that the child care agency may encounter in seeking to place a deaf child with a deaf family is the shortage of deaf applicants. As a result of the negative messages deaf people receive from hearing people (mostly implicit, but some quite explicit, as outlined earlier) many deaf families with the capacity to foster or adopt will be reluctant to come forward for fear of further rejection. The possibility of fostering or adopting is rarely, if ever, discussed in Deaf clubs and many deaf adults have assumed that they would not be eligible since the 'rules' are usually made by hearing people. Specific publicity will therefore be needed to encourage deaf families to apply.

The most common form of publicity is an advertisement in the deaf media (for example, *British Deaf News*, *Talk*, *Talking Sense* or the Teletext pages, 'No Need to Shout' and 'Ear Shot') for a family for a particular child. We give some examples of these in Appendix V. Sadly, some of these advertisements serve only to clarify for deaf people the level of ignorance of the issues within the placing agency. For example, failure to mention or a condescending reference to the child's mode of communication will throw into doubt the agency's commitment to finding a deaf family. Too much written content will discourage many deaf adults who have difficulty in deciphering written language. A good quality picture and a few clear sentences about the child and the agency's aims for him or her are likely to maximise the effectiveness.

Access to the Deaf Community

Advertisements alone however, will have only a limited effect. An agency or social worker committed to finding a deaf family will need to make more active approaches to the Deaf Community. For most child care workers who have a limited knowledge of the issues of deafness this will mean working closely with colleagues who have these skills and with deaf people. To gain access to a local Deaf club is important, but access will only be useful if careful thought is put into making the best use of it.

Guaranteed confidentiality

Interpreters and careful preparation of material will be needed. It is important to recognise that deaf people have the same need for privacy and the same reluctance to expose themselves as any other people. Arrangements should be made to ensure that potential applicants can be interviewed in private with an appropriate interpreter present. Many deaf adults have expressed doubts about the protection of confidentiality and have given this as a reason for their reluctance to come forward. The Deaf Community is small and many effective 'grapevines' operate. The agency may therefore need to 'buy in' interpreting skills from outside the immediate community to guarantee confidentiality.

Television and video

Television is, of course, an important medium for deaf people. There are several programmes specifically for deaf viewers and some have already demonstrated their willingness to feature children needing families and to open up the debate about the advantages of deaf foster and adoptive families for deaf children in care. The staff of these programmes are experts in communication and are therefore a very valuable source of advice and guidance on how to get the message across most effectively.

Any video made about a deaf child should, wherever possible, contain a Sign Language interpretation, and this principle could be extended to any recruitment and training material on video which the agency may use. In addition to making the material intelligible to deaf people, this will be seen as further evidence of the agency's commitment to the recruitment of deaf families.

Preparation groups
It is unlikely that any one child care agency will have sufficient need for deaf families to justify the regular running of preparation groups specifically for them. A single programme of such groups may, however, be appropriate, or a regular programme could be shared among several agencies in one region. However, where this is done it is important that travel is facilitated and, as with all appplicants, the costs are met by the recruiting agency.

In most cases preparation programmes for deaf prospective adoptive and foster families will be undertaken in mixed deaf and hearing groups. The content of the programmes will need to be reviewed to ensure that they are intelligible to deaf people. At the very least, deaf people should be provided with interpreters during the sessions but care must also be taken to ensure that written material is clear and videos have signed translations. The lighting in the room should be good enough to facilitate lip-reading and care should be taken with the seating arrangements to ensure maximum visibility. At least one agency has a loop system installed in its meeting room to facilitate those with sufficient residual hearing to follow discussions and to hear videos. A Deaf Communicating Terminal for the telephone is a small investment for an agency and would also be helpful.

The examples of cases given in the preparation process should be appropriate, or at least be introduced in a way that demonstrates an awareness of the sensitivity of the issues for deaf participants. The use of audio tapes should be avoided when there are deaf members of the group unless they can be fully and satisfactorily interpreted. Role play can be effective (if interpreted) but thought needs to be given to the adaptation of this and other training methods.

The selection process
The process of selecting deaf foster and adoptive families should not differ greatly from that of selecting other such families, although the child care social workers will probably need some help from people knowledgeable about the issues of deafness. The family's attitude to

deafness, its mode of communication and links with the Deaf and hearing communities will be relevant to the selection process.

There is no need to change in any way the criteria for linking the child and family, since the use of a deaf family for a deaf child is a better way of meeting some of that child's identified needs. In the same way, a black child is still best placed in a black family and a child with multiple disabilities in a family which can cope with and positively benefit from caring for such a child. If the black child or the child with disabilities is also deaf then suitable families should first be sought within the Deaf Community.

Access to support systems

Foster and adoptive families caring for deaf children will, like all others, need the support systems necessary for successful family placements – child care social workers, doctors, teachers, fellow carers and others. But deaf families will also need ways of accessing such help. The placing agency may need to provide an interpreter, as well as a social worker who is able to communicate directly with the family. Above all, it is vital that the child should have a social worker with whom he or she can communicate.

A problem for many agencies will be the current shortage of trained social workers who are skilled in Sign Language and who also have a good knowledge of child care and substitute family care. One way around this is for the specialist social worker with deaf people and the child care worker to work together, although this has some disadvantages. In the long term, larger agencies, or those (probably voluntary agencies) who seek to specialise in the placement of deaf children could ensure that at least one member of the child care team has communication skills and a knowledge of deaf issues. Consistent co-working with the social worker with deaf people or interpreter will facilitate understanding of each other's knowledge and skills. In the interim, the full and informed use of interpreters and in particular the creative use of deaf volunteers in the preparation and support services will help to ensure that deaf children are not disadvantaged by the agency's shortcomings.

Sign Language courses should be offered at the agency's expense to close members of the extended family or friends if this will help the child in the placement.

Deaf families could also benefit from contact with other deaf foster and adoptive parents. At present the number of such families is small and they are so widely spread across the British Isles that physical contact may prove impossible, but this is a possibility to be considered.

The Deaf Community could also be encouraged to produce volunteers to help deaf children in care in a number of imaginative ways. These could include activities for the child, participation in the preparation and support services for the family, and an educative role with others members of the Deaf Community and an advocate role for the child.

The resources of the Deaf Community

The Deaf Community contains many resources which agencies cannot afford to overlook if they are genuinely seeking to provide the best for the deaf children entrusted to their care. A senior social worker in a fostering/adoption team wrote to the working party about her experience of a Deaf couple who had adopted two deaf children: 'The whole family moves easily between the Deaf world and the hearing world. Their communication successes are excellent.' The first child was placed with them as a two-year-old: 'He had a traumatic history of non-accidental injury, was totally unable to communicate and the adoption proceedings were long drawn out and contested. The family coped right from the start and the boy developed into an intelligent, secure and lively child who has thrived in all areas of his development, particularly in his communication skills.'

However, she noted that the family had waited five years before a child was placed with them and feared that: 'unless we, as social workers, are prepared to overcome our apparent prejudices against deafness, and actually use the families [and] . . . unless social workers themselves are trained and prepared to accept that the Deaf Community has the positive skills and experiences appropriate to helping deaf children in care . . . [then] a move to recruit more widely from the Deaf Community, building up a family's hope that it can adopt, is unfair.'

Voluntary organisations in the field of deafness and hearing impairment provide services for deaf children and social workers and families concerned with their care. Amongst these are national bodies identified with specific membership groups such as parents of deaf children, profoundly deaf adults, hard-of-hearing people and families of deaf-blind children. Others seek to provide a range of services for a broad spectrum of deaf and hearing-impaired people of all ages and some groups focus on particular types of activity. We list the principal organisations in Appendix III.

References

1 Higgins P *Outsiders in a hearing world – a sociology of deafness* Beverly Hills California: Sage Publications, 1980.

Appendix 1   Glossary of terms

Adenoids	These are tissues situated at the back of the nose where it joins to the roof of the throat. They lie at the opening of the Eustachian tube and when enlarged may obstruct both the back of the nose and the Eustachian tube.
Acquired deafness	Often referred to as either 'deafened', 'post-lingual' or 'adventitious' deafness – where a person becomes deaf after acquiring speech and verbal language.
Audiogram	A graph showing the degree of hearing impairment in terms of frequency (Hertz) and loudness (decibels).
Audiologist	A person with professional qualifications in the assessment and management of hearing impairment and disability.
British Sign Language (BSL)	The language of the Deaf Community in Britain. It is a complete visual gestural language.
Cochlea	The part of the inner ear which changes sound energy into electrical impulses which are then passed on to the brain via the auditory nerve.
Cochlear implant	A special type of hearing aid where an electrode is placed surgically in the inner ear. It is only suitable for people who cannot hear anything through conventional hearing aids.
Conductive deafness	Results from a problem either in the outer or middle ear which prevents sound energy being passed on to the inner ear.
Congenital deafness	Deafness present at birth.
Cued speech	A one-handed supplement to spoken language to assist with words or sounds that are ambiguous or invisible in lip-reading.
Deaf/Blind Manual	A system of spelling out words on the receiver's hand.
Deafened	See Acquired deafness.

DCT	A Deaf Communicating Terminal is an appliance resembling a small personal computer which used in conjunction with a telephone enables deaf people to contact each other. The equipment has a visual display on which the typed conversation appears. Brand names include Minicom and Vistel.
Decibel	A unit of measure of loudness.
Deaf without speech	DHSS definitions for the purpose of registration by social services under welfare legislation: 'those who have no useful hearing and whose normal method of communication is by signs, finger spelling or writing.'
Deaf with speech	– 'those who (even with a hearing aid) have little or no useful hearing but whose normal method of communication is by speech and lip-reading.'
ENT	An abbreviation for ear, nose and throat. It is usually used as an adjective to describe a surgeon, a hospital department or a clinic.
Eustachian tube	A tube connecting the middle ear to the back of the nose and roof of the throat. It allows air to enter the middle ear.
Education Act 1981	A major piece of legislation which allows for multidisciplinary assessment and legal statementing of a child's special educational needs, with advice being submitted by various professionals and by the parents.
Familial deafness	see Hereditary deafness.
Genetic counselling	Advice given which is based on inherited features. Often given to prospective parents when the risk of producing a child with a given set of inherited physical features is assessed.
German measles	see Rubella.
Glue ear	Also known as chronic otitis media or serious otitis media. A common condition in the pre-school and young school-aged child, where fluid accumulates in the middle ear producing a conductive hearing loss.

Grommet	A tiny tube which is surgically inserted across the ear drum to dry out the fluid which has accumulated in the middle ear space in glue ear.
Hands on communication	Sign language is used by the communicator. The receiver (deaf-blind person) feels through contact what is being communicated.
Hearing aids	Sophisticated technological appliances worn at the ear or on the body as a means of making sounds louder for the hearing-impaired.
Hereditary deafness	Deafness that is passed on from one generation to another through the genes. The parents of a child with hereditary deafness may not necessarily be deaf themselves eg Usher Syndrome.
Hearing impairment	Often the generic term for deafness, though many people use it to distinguish those who are deafened or partially hearing from those who are profoundly deaf.
Hard of hearing	A term describing people who have a moderate to severe hearing loss who may rely on the use of hearing aids and lip-reading. DHSS definition for the purpose of registration by social services under welfare legislation: 'those who (with or without a hearing aid) have some useful hearing and whose normal method of communication is by speech, and lip-reading.'
Impedance test	A method of measuring the movement of the ear drum, particularly useful for detecting glue ear.
Jaundice	A medical condition which may result in deafness if the jaundice at the time of birth is very severe.
KiloHertz (Hz)	1000 Hertz (Hz). Hertz is a measure of sound frequency.
Lip-reading (or Speech-reading)	A communication method whereby hearing-impaired people combine the sounds they hear with the lip-patterns of the speaker. As many shapes of words are invisible or indistinguishable from others, the lip-reader relies on the context in which the words occur and a good deal of guesswork.

Loop system	An amplifier and a looped length of wire which, through a microphone, enables sound from a television, radio, persons speaking, etc to be sent direct to a hearing aid with a 'T' setting.
Makaton	A specially selected vocabulary of signs from BSL useful in providing basic communication. Nowadays it is generally restricted to use with people with severe learning difficulties.
Mastoiditis	An infection of the mastoid air cells in the mastoid bone situated in the skull behind the ear.
Middle ear	Situated inside the head and responsible for the transmission of sound waves from the ear drum to the oval window. It measures less than half an inch.
Moulds	Usually referred to as earmoulds, these are the part of the hearing aid equipment which fits into the ear canal.
Nerve deafness	see Sensori-neural deafness.
Ossicles	The three tiny bones in the middle ear.
Oral/aural	A communication method which focuses on the use of lip-reading and reliance on hearing aid where the promotion of speech is seen as an essential aim.
Otolaryngologist	An ear, nose and throat specialist.
Paget Gorman	A generated sign system which gives simultaneous signed grammatical representation of spoken English.
Peripatetic teacher (of the deaf)	A teacher employed by the LEA to make home visits. They are particularly involved with pre-school deaf children.
Pre-lingually deaf	There is now agreement on the term –generally it is used to describe someone who was either born deaf or who became deaf in very early infancy before the development of spoken language.

Radio aid	A special technological appliance which allows a radio transmission of a speaker's voice to be picked up by a receiver worn by a hearing-impaired person. The receiver worn by the hearing-impaired person may also incorporate a hearing aid, but is not usually used with the person's own hearing aids. This system is particularly useful in classroom situations or where there is a lot of background noise.
Rubella	Also known as German measles. A mild and common childhood illness, which if caught by a pregnant mother can cause widespread damage, including deafness to her baby.
Sensori-neural deafness	Deafness resulting from damage to the inner ear (sensory) or to the nerve of hearing (neural). It is not curable by medical or surgical treatment.
Sign supported English	Signs from BSL used simultaneously with grammatically spoken English.
Signed English	BSL signs and other generated signs and markers used to give an exact signed representation of spoken English.
Statements	An LEA is required to make an assessment of the 'special educational needs' of any children that have been referred to it by the medical authorities. Once assessment is complete a statement of both the child's educational needs and the proposed provision is set out formally on paper. This is a Statement.
Total communication	A communication and educational method deploying more than one of the following: gestures, Sign Language, speech, finger-spelling, and use of hearing aids.
Traumatic deafness	When a person is deafened by injury to the head, explosion or blast, or illness, eg meningitis. Onset of deafness is sudden.
Usher Syndrome	A cause of inherited congenital deafness with some associated loss of vision which usually occurs in the early teens and which may worsen with age.

Appendix II
Questionnaire on deaf children in local authority care

Questionnaire sent to all 127 social services authorities in Great Britain in January 1989.

Using the following definitions of *deafness* and *children to be included* please answer the questions as fully as possible. Nil returns are also important.

Deafness

(a) *Partially hearing:* may also be described as moderately or severely hearing-impaired (records may show a hearing loss of up to about 70dB). These children may attend mainstream or special schools/units and some may wear hearing aids.

(b) *Profoundly deaf:* many of these children will have little residual hearing but may also wear hearing aids. They will be more likely to be in a special educational setting. Records may show a hearing loss of 70dB and upwards. They are more likely (than partially hearing children) to use gesture and signs and to have difficulty with spoken language.

NB Some partially hearing and profoundly deaf children have additional disabilities. Please include these with the total numbers in columns (a) **or** (b) and in (c) **or** (d).

Children to be included

Those on Statutory or Voluntary orders who are permanently or temporarily unable to live with their own families. (*Do not* include children home on trial).

1) How many partially hearing or profoundly deaf children are in your local authority care?

2) Where are they living?
    ● with relatives
    ● with foster parents – long term
    – short term
    ● with prospective adoptive family
    ● in children's home
    ● in residential school (52 weeks per year)
    ● in hospital
    ● elsewhere – please specify

3) How many are awaiting foster or adoptive families?

4) How many are
    – black (*including African, Caribbean & Asian*)
    – other ethnic minority
    – white

5) How many are with at least one foster/prospective adoptive parent who is partially hearing or profoundly deaf?

TOTAL		Of the children in cols a/b how many have additional disabilities?	
a	b	c	d
Partially hearing	Profoundly deaf	Partially hearing	Profoundly deaf

Appendix III Organisations supporting deaf people

The British Deaf Association (BDA)

The BDA is the national membership organisation of the Deaf Community. Most of its 18,000 members were born deaf or became deaf in childhood and use British Sign Language (BSL). The Association's policies and priorities are determined by Deaf people through a structure of branches established in most local Deaf clubs, regional councils, a National Executive Council and Annual Delegates Conference.

Users of the BDA's information, advice and advocacy services are primarily Deaf people and their families and professional workers. The majority of enquiries concern issues involving Sign Language and interpreting, education, social work services, and discrimination against Deaf people.

The BDA gives particular emphasis to identifying and developing the abilities and potential of Deaf people to serve their own and the wider community.

In association with the University of Durham it has established qualifying training for Deaf people as tutors of BSL and maintains a register of local Sign Language courses. With statutory and voluntary youth organisations, it is developing training and support for Deaf part-time youth workers and opportunities for youth and community work in order to increase and improve access to youth services for young deaf people.

The Association offers self-catering family holidays at holiday flats in Bridlington and funds its affiliated body, the British Deaf Sports Council, to administer the largest programmes of 'disabled' sport at regional, national and international levels.

The BDA's monthly magazine, *The British Deaf News*, is a primary source of information and news for the Deaf Community and is widely read by social workers with deaf people. Information videos presented in Sign Language are produced on a range of subjects and reports and other publications are available on subjects including education, Sign Language and discrimination.

The National Deaf Children's Society (NDCS)

The National Deaf Children's Society represents the interests of deaf and partially hearing children and their families. It provides a headquarters-based advice, advocacy and counselling service on education, health and welfare issues. Courses and conferences are arranged for parents and professionals and an annual festival of performing arts for deaf children.

The Society's Technology Information Centre (TIC) in Birmingham operates a lending library of radio hearing aids and demonstrates and offers expert advice on the increasing applications of technology of benefit to deaf people.

NDCS gives specialist equipment to individual children and schools and welfare grants to families. In addition, publications on specific subjects, the quarterly magazine *Talk* and the *NDCS Year Book*, which includes a comprehensive directory of educational provision for the British Isles, are particularly useful to families and professional workers.

Local NDCS groups around the country provide essential mutual support for parents and are a ready source of information about local services and contact with teachers of the deaf and specialist social workers, who are often members.

SENSE (The National Deaf-Blind and Rubella Association)

Families supporting deaf-blind and multiply-disabled deaf children make up the membership of SENSE. A Family Advisory Service operates through centres in London, Birmingham, Newcastle and Glasgow. It provides a home-visiting service; parent-child weekend courses; parents' weekend workshops; individual developmental assessment days; specialist advice, particularly on educational needs; courses for parents and professional workers; support for teachers working with deaf-blind children; and opportunities for parents to meet other parents. The Service has teachers, physiotherapists and other specialist workers who have all had experience in working with the young deaf-blind or multiply-disabled child. It will respond to requests for help and advice from parents and professional workers anywhere in the country. Three further education and rehabilitation establishments, in Birmingham, Peterborough and Glasgow, provide vital post-school social education and training for deaf-blind young adults. SENSE also runs a holiday programme for deaf-blind children and young people.

The Association's publications include research and information material on rubella and Usher Syndrome (the two common causes of deaf-blindness) and the quarterly magazine *Talking Sense*.

The British Association of the Hard of Hearing (BAHOH)

The British Association of the Hard of Hearing is a membership organisation primarily serving those who lose all or part of their hearing after acquiring speech and language and who communicate using residual hearing, hearing aids and lip-reading.

BAHOH administers the Sympathetic Hearing Scheme which promotes informed attitudes and clear communication with hearing-impaired customers by staff in shops, banks and other retail, commercial and public sector service points. The majority of members of BAHOH's 200 affiliated local clubs are older adults, but the Association has a developing programme of involvement and activity for young hearing-impaired people. An advice and information service is supported by publications on services, aspects of oral/aural communication and the quarterly magazine *Hark*.

Breakthrough Trust (Deaf-Hearing Integration)

The cornerstone of Breakthrough's work is the promotion of communication in its widest sense and by every available means in order to achieve greater interaction and understanding between deaf, hearing-impaired and hearing people. The organisation provides services from its main base in Birmingham including a communication training, counselling and resource centre. Projects in London, Farnborough and at the Roughmoor Centre near Swindon offer similar services, whilst Roughmoor is also widely used for courses and holidays for many integrated groups. Breakthrough pioneered the introduction and development of Deaf Communicating Terminals in Britain and maintains a keen involvement in the use of telecommunications by deaf people. It has developed particular experience in work with multiply-disabled deaf children through integrated holidays and special activity groups.

Friends of the Young Deaf (FYD)

Friends of the Young Deaf is notable for its recognition of the potential for self-help amongst hearing-impaired young people. Through its work in confidence building, skills teaching and teamwork, FYD has evolved a programme for developing leadership and organisational skills which have enabled young people to identify and meet their own needs for social, recreational and sporting activity.

The Royal National Institute for the Deaf (RNID)

The services of the Royal National Institute for the Deaf reflect its concern with hearing impairment from moderate hearing loss to profound deafness, and associated problems such as deaf-blindness and tinnitus. A large lending library and information service gives access to an extensive range of books and other publications. The RNID *Information Directory*, published annually, is particularly useful and includes a comprehensive listing of social services, education, health and voluntary organisations relating to deafness.

RNID residential and training facilities include provision for young deaf people with particular problems and special needs at several centres in England.

The technology of communication from hearing aids and aids to daily living (environmental aids) to electronic mail is a particular area of resources and expertise and the RNID provides advice and information from its London headquarters and a base in Glasgow. Its Telephone Exchange for the Deaf enables deaf people using DCTs and electronic mail to communicate with any telephone subscriber.

Regional staff in Manchester, Nottingham, Birmingham, Bath and London, who have extensive knowledge of services in their areas, are concerned with the promotion and development of statutory and voluntary services. Awareness training programmes are provided in response to the needs of workers in many professions who come into contact with deaf people.

Appendix IV   Diagram of the ear

Adapted with kind permission from 'medical aspects of deafness' leaflet designed by Jill Mansfield for AVTS (Audio-Visual Training Services, 30 Stonehouse Park, Thursby, Carlisle CA5 6NS).

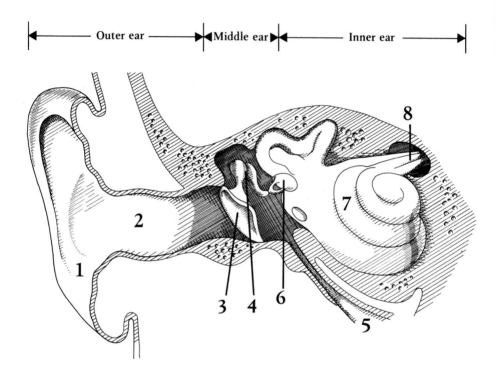

The outer ear and middle ear conduct sound waves from the outer world to the inner ear. Any faults here give rise to 'conductive' deafness. The cochlea and auditory nerve which form the inner ear are responsible for 'sensing' the sound signals and transmitting them to the brain. Any problems in the inner ear give rise to what is known as 'sensori-neural' deafness.

1 Auricle or pinna

This is shaped so that it picks up sound waves and passes them down into the ear canal.

2 Ear canal or external auditory meatus

Sound waves pass along here until they reach the ear drum. If there is any obstruction such as wax or foreign bodies (eg something put into the ear by a child or a forgotten plug of wool) sound waves will not be able to pass along so well. Fortunately these obstructions can usually be removed quite easily. Another problem is the blockage cause by swelling of the ear canal due to infection.

3 Ear drum or tympanum

When the sound waves reach this, they cause it to vibrate and then transmit the sound to the next part of the ear.

The ear drum can be damaged in a number of ways, such as by a blow to the head, by an explosion causing sudden extreme pressure in the ear, by careless syringing or probing, or by infection. All these can cause rupture or perforation of the drum which reduces its ability to vibrate. Sometimes perforations can be closed by a graft.

4 Ossicles

These are little bones situated in the middle ear, which is an air-filled chamber. There are three of them and the first, the hammer or malleus, is attached to the ear drum. Vibrations of the ear drum are transferred to the hammer which then passes them on to the second ossicle, the anvil or incus. This in turn passes them on to the third ossicle, the stirrup (or stapes).

Head injury or disease can reduce or completely stop the vibrations being passed along the 'chain'. The ossicles can either be damaged as in otosclerosis, a disease which causes them to harden or seize up; or their movement may be restricted by fluid in the middle ear, as in 'glue ear', or by debris caused by infection (cholesteatoma). Otitis media, also caused by infection, gives rise to problems due to inflammation and swelling. Many of the problems causing middle ear deafness can be cured by antibiotics (otitis media) or by surgery (glue ear, otosclerosis, cholesteatoma formation).

5 Eustachian tube

This is a passage from the nose which enables air to reach the middle ear. Any obstruction here will cause the air pressure in the middle ear to fall, so that the ear drum is drawn inwards and its ability to vibrate is dampened. Fluid may develop if the obstruction is not relieved. Catarrh may obstruct the tube temporarily during a head cold.

6 Oval window

This is a delicate, flexible membrane which is attached to the last ossicle, the stapes, from which vibrations are transferred.

7 Cochlea

So called because of its similarity to a snail shell, the cochlea is like a coiled tube and is filled with fluid. The vibration of the oval window causes sound waves to be transmitted to the fluid and a wave-like ripple passes along the tube. This causes a vibration of thousands of 'hair cells' situated along the length of the tube. These vibrations start the chain of nerve impulses which carries sound information to the brain.

8 Auditory (hearing) nerve

This transmits nerve impulses from the hair cells in the cochlea and passes the 'message' to the auditory cortex or brain.

Faults in the cochlea and auditory nerve which form the inner ear can be due to infections such as mumps, measles and meningitis; drugs known to be 'ototoxic'; deterioration of the hearing mechanism due to age; or over-exposure to noise such as loud music, road drills, industrial noise, gunfire, farm machinery, etc. Damage to any part of the inner ear can rarely be cured.

Appendix V Advertisements for foster and adoptive parents for deaf children

Photographs of the children have not been reproduced in these examples (to maximise their effectiveness, adverts should feature a good quality picture of the child). We are grateful to the agencies concerned for permission to reproduce the wording of these advertisements.

If you are a parent who is deaf or hard of hearing and are interested in fostering, read on

Alan is 12 years of age. He is profoundly deaf, partially sighted and developmentally delayed. Alan has lived most of his life in a Children's Home and has had no contact with his natural parents since birth.

Alan is generally contented and easy going, and enjoyable to be with. He can equally be an energetic, lively boy who enjoys individual attention. He likes to be outdoors, particularly on swings, is a good swimmer and has a mischievous sense of fun. Alan walks well, is able to dress himself, apart from the buttons, go to the toilet and eat by himself.

Alan now needs a family, couple or single person, of his own who would have an overall commitment to him, but who initially could care for him during school holidays. Since September this year Alan has been attending a boarding school.

Although Alan has only been at the school for a short period of time he has already made good progress and has the potential to learn many new skills. He needs a family who would be able to help him to do things for himself. As he is unable to speak or hear, Alan needs people who will be able to make themselves understood, and who would be able to provide him with security in his new surroundings. Alan has had teaching in Makaton and knows a few signs, but his ability to communicate is an area that needs to be concentrated on in future.

[The worker's name and agency address and contact details have been omitted.]

Could you be Michelle's foster family?

Michelle is 13 years old. She is profoundly deaf and has a mental disability. Although she attends a school well suited to her special requirements, she desperately needs a family of her own.

Michelle can be a gentle, loving person and fun to be with, as she is very lively and has a mischievous sense of humour. She loves energetic games and wearing flowing clothes and dangly beads. She is also a loner, playing obsessively, with little interest in other people. She is very strong and can sometimes hit out in a temper.

Michelle is quite good at looking after herself and can use simple Sign Language. She could not cope outside on her own.

Maybe you have special knowledge and experience which could make you the right family for Michelle?

If you live in Kent or within easy travelling distance of London, please contact (worker's name) at the Norfolk Adoption and Family Finding Unit, Norwich NR2 2PA, telephone Norwich (0603) 617796, who will be glad to tell you more.

BOBBY

Bobby is a lively six-year-old of mixed parentage (white/Asian). He is energetic and so can be demanding, but is an affectionate and rewarding child to care for.

Bobby attends a partially-hearing unit where he is making very good progress. He wears two hearing aids.

We are looking for an Asian family living outside Lambeth who reflect Bobby's Hindu background.

Bobby needs to be in a family where other children are much older or younger than himself.

Financial assistance may be available.

Interested? Contact (worker's name) or cut out this advert and send it to: Lambeth Family Finders, 392 Brixton Road, London SW9 7AW.

Name

Address

Phone

Please tell me more about
☐ Bobby ☐ Fostering ☐ Adoption

Appendix VI   Useful addresses

Organisations which can offer information, advice, support and other services to fostering/adoption workers and substitute families with regard to the needs of deaf children and those with multiple disabilities.

Breakthrough (Deaf-Hearing Integration) Trust
Charles W Gillet Centre
Selly Oak Colleges
Birmingham B29 6LE

British Association of the Hard of Hearing
7-11 Armstrong Road
London W3 7JL

British Deaf Association
38 Victoria Place
Carlisle CA1 1HU

Contact-a-Family
16 Stutton Ground
London SW1

Family Fund
PO Box 50
York YO1 1UY

Friends of the Young Deaf
FYD Communication Centre
East Court Mansion
College Lane
East Grinstead
Sussex

Invalid Children's Aid Association
126 Buckingham Palace Road
London SW1

National Deaf Children's Society
45 Hereford Road
London W2 5AH

National Toy Libraries Association
Play Matters
68 Churchway
London NW1 1LT

Royal National Institute for the Blind
224 Great Portland Street
London W1

Royal National Institute for the Deaf
105 Gower Street
London WC1 6AH

SENSE (The National Deaf-Blind and Rubella Association)
311 Grays Inn Road
London WC1X 8PT

Spastics Society
12 Park Crescent
London W1

Appendix VII   Bibliography

Available from BAAF (British Agencies for Adoption & Fostering)

Macaskill C *Against the odds: adopting mentally handicapped children* BAAF, 1985.

Rushton A, Treseder J and Quinton D *New parents for older children* BAAF, 1988.

Sawbridge P (ed) *Parents for children: twelve practice papers* BAAF, 1983.

Wedge P and Thoburn J (eds) *Finding families for 'hard-to-place' children: evidence from research* BAAF, 1986.

Available from the BDA (British Deaf Association)

Grant B (ed) *The quiet ear: deafness in literature* Andre Deutsch, 1987.

Mindel E and D and Vernon M *They grow in silence: the deaf child and his family* National Association of the Deaf (USA), 1987.

Spradley T and J *Deaf like me* Random House, 1978.

Reports

Raise the standard: the case for improving deaf children's education BDA, 1985.

BSL: Britain's fourth language BDA, 1987.

Occasional papers

Bellugi U 'Attitudes towards Sign Language' *The British Deaf News* October 1976.

Merrill E 'A deaf presence in education' *The British Deaf News* August 1979.

Merrill E 'Education of the prelingually deaf child' *The British Deaf News* June 1981.

Merrill E 'The responsibilities of professionals to the deaf consumer' *The British Deaf News* December 1976.

Montgomery G 'Changing attitudes to communication' *The British Deaf News* June 1976.

Montgomery G 'Effective brains v defective ears' *The British Deaf News* July 1980.

Moore M 'Total Communication' *The British Deaf News* August 1978.

Norden K 'Deaf family life: growing-up conditions for deaf children of deaf or hearing parents and hearing children of deaf parents' *The British Deaf News* February 1978.

Sheavyn M 'Why I changed my mind' *The British Deaf News* December 1979.

Available from NDCS (National Deaf Children's Society)

Reports

Always a step behind NDCS, 1987 (2nd edition 1989). Describes the difficulties faced by children with acquired deafness.

The missing link NDCS, 1988. The effect of the 1981 Education Act on deaf children and services from health authorities.

Available from SENSE (National Deaf-Blind and Rubella Association)

Best A *Steps to independence* BIMH Publications, 1987.

Brock M *Christopher: a silent life* Bedford Square Press, 1984.

Dale F *Progress guide for deaf-blind and/or severely handicapped children* SENSE, 1977.

Freeman P *The deaf-blind baby: a programme of care* Heinemann, 1985.

Freeman P *A parent's guide to the early care of a deaf-blind child* SENSE, 1971.

Usher Syndrome awareness and education pack SENSE, 1988.

Available from bookshops and publishers

British Sign Language: a beginner's guide BBC Books, 1988.

Fletcher L *A Language for Ben: a deaf child's right to sign* Souvenir Press, 1987.

Kyle J and Woll B *Sign Language: the study of deaf people and their language* Cambridge University Press, 1985.

Lane H *When the mind hears: a history of the deaf* Souvenir Press, 1984.

Mencher G and Gerber S (eds) *The multiply handicapped hearing-impaired child* Grune and Stratton, 1984.

The multi-handicapped hearing-impaired: identification and instruction Washington DC: Gallaudet College Press, 1982.

Nolan M and Tucker I *The hearing-impaired child and the family* Souvenir Press, 1981.

Sacks O *Seeing voices* Picador, 1990.

Wyman R *Multiply handicapped children* Souvenir Press, 1986.

Appendix VIII Videography

Available from BAAF (British Agencies for Adoption & Fostering)

Whose handicap? BAAF, 1986. Finding new families for children with mental disabilities.

Available from BAHOH (British Association of the Hard of Hearing)

The sympathetic hearing scheme BAHOH, 1983.

Available from BBC Publications

British Sign Language: a beginner's guide BBC, 1988. Based on the ten-part BBC-TV series.

Available from the BDA (British Deaf Association)

The Christmas Story BDA, 1987. Presented in Sign Language with voice-over.

Contraception BDA, 1985. Signed English presentation.

Having a baby BDA, 1985. BSL presentation with voice-over.

See, Say, Sign series, BDA, 1984. BSL or Signed English presentation with voice-over of stories, mainly from Ladybird books, for children:

1 Billy Goats Gruff
   Three Little Pigs
   Cinderella

2 Three stories from Aesop's Fables
   Four nursery rhymes
   Silly Jack

3 Hansel and Gretel
   The old woman and her pig
   The house that Jack built

What is BSL? BDA, 1986. BSL presentation with voice-over.

Available from NDCS (National Deaf Children's Society)

Listening through frosted glass NDCS, 1987.

One in a thousand: the work of the NDCS NDCS, 1985.

Special needs, special choices NDCS, 1987. A look at the five most popular methods used in the education of deaf children.

Available from SENSE (National Deaf-Blind and Rubella Association)

Development in young deaf-blind children SENSE, 1989.

The gift and sight of hearing SENSE, 1988.

Keeping in touch SENSE, 1989. Looks at Usher Syndrome.

Principles: teaching deaf-blind children SENSE, 1989.

The quiet tunnel SENSE, 1986. Looks at Usher Syndrome.

Using residual vision SENSE, 1989.